**Change is supported under grants
from the Esso Education and Ford Foundations**

The essays in this book have all appeared in
Change Magazine

INSIDE   ACADEME

—

CULTURE IN CRISIS

Edited by the editors of *Change*

CONTENTS

About the Authors

George W. Bonham is editor-in-chief of *Change* Magazine.

Kate Haracz is a graduate student in sociology. She wrote her undergraduate journal while a junior at James Madison College, Michigan State University.

Irvin Stock is professor of English at the University of Massachusetts in Boston. He is the author of *William Hale White (Mark Rutherford): A Critical Study,* and *Mary MacArthur* in the American Writers' Series. He has also produced off-Broadway plays.

Franklin Chu, a graduate of Harvard College, served as an editor of the *Harvard Crimson* and the *Harvard Lampoon.*

Benjamin DeMott, an essayist and novelist, teaches English at Amherst College, Massachusetts.

Michael Rossman was a leading figure in the 1969 Free Speech Movement at Berkeley. An expanded version of his article will appear in his "On Learning and Social Change," published in late 1972.

Andrew M. Greeley is the director of the Center for the Study of American Pluralism, University of Chicago.

David Riesman is professor of social relations at Harvard University, and currently on leave at The Institute for Advanced Study at Princeton University.

Edgar Z. Friedenberg is professor of sociology at Dalhousie University, Halifax, Nova Scotia.

Ruth Hawkins, a member of the National Organization for Women, is the social science editor with the Educational Development Corporation in Palo Alto, California.

Nathan Glazer, professor of education and social structure at Harvard University's School of Education, is currently on leave at the Center for Advanced Study in the Behavioral Sciences in Stanford, California.

Arthur M. Cohen and Florence B. Brawer are on the staff of the Graduate School of Education at the University of California at Los Angeles. Professor Cohen serves as the director of the ERIC Clearinghouse for Junior College Information.

Michael Maccoby, a psychoanalyst, is a fellow at the Institute for Policy Studies in Washington, where he is directing a project on Technology, Work and Character, sponsored by Harvard University's Program on Technology and Society.

Inside Academe

by George W. Bonham

When historians finally write their chapter on 20th century American higher education, the more prescient of them may well mark the sixties as higher learning's dark night of the soul. Much of this book dwells deeply with this dark night, and the first glimmer of a new dawn. Attacked from within and discredited from without, the academy has of late come to look like a cultural battleground from which some of the main combatants may never return. There are many survivors, but few will ever be the same again.

As with so many other hallowed public institutions, our colleges and universities fell victims to their own historicity. Virtuously committed to the self-perpetuation of academic dogma and class, encapsulated by the past rather than by the present and future, and dealing comfortably with life with the hygienic scalpels of pedagogy and scholarship, they were in no way prepared for the postwar's cultural transformation and for the general acceleration of life.

Higher education came to be both the victim and an accessory of the enormous discontinuities which vast cultural change had mercilessly left in its wake. Even the most talented academic men and women could not know, nor did they really try to understand, how to behave under such changed circumstances, aside from continuing to do what had worked before. Nor did most see their role in any sense connected with the larger cultural cataclysms which deeply embroiled a nation in a crisis of conscience and performance. It was easy enough to separate learning from action. *Let society change as it may. We shall study it in good time.*

What was worse, academics had long assumed themselves to be essential anchorpoints of social progress, a case which no one thought again needed to be proven. But among the many virtues of the academic and intellectual class the power of self-delusion is not one. To connect the passions of one's mind to the new secular realities struck many as entirely foreign, hardly worthy of academic dispassion and scholarship.

It is, or course, this very separation of knowledge and consequent retreat, from social reality and social conscience that has aroused the young, and which has shaken the confidence in education of those who make the decisions in terms of the universities' and colleges' future. But while we wallow in our own ambivalence on such matters, it is important to remember what is worth preserving and what is not. It is still the academics who should have a better sense of such measures, for only they can in the main afford the luxury of the daily celebration of one's mind. And if the promised roadway still lies enshrouded in the mist of uncertainty, one can begin at least with a sense of direction.

To what degree we can expect the academic to sense the right directions remains to be seen. In calmer and more halcyon days, educators were thought to be an effective gyroscope by which social stability and improvement were to be measured. But our sense of what is vital and what is trivial has of late become distorted. Such relationships of values remain to be sorted out and placed in some kind of systemic framework. That this has not yet been achieved is seen by much recent calamitous evidence. One day we pay wholesale obeisance to the omniscence of youth, and condemn it the next. We bow to the cry of "relevance" and abandon all concern for cerebral excellence in the process. We think one day of education as being infallible to social criticism, and the next flaggelate ourselves mercilessly for our egregious failures. Today we make much of academic freedom, and tomorrow violate it by outrageous individual behavior in a way which no ordinary citizen would tolerate.

And often, an affronting layer of academic hubris covers it all.

So for the moment, that once useful gyroscope is due for some fevered gyrations of its own. But beneath all of this turmoil, there now emerges a new spirit on our campuses and a new resolve to successfully deal with our young, with each other and with life, in quite new and more honest ways. These new pathways remain blurred and still unconnected. Yot, they are now being forged in the minds and hearts of many remarkable men and women on campuses all over the country. Some day they will all connect and transform higher learning into something quite remarkable and more essential to national life.

The twelve essays in this book confirm this sense of passion and commitment. All search for answers that go far beyond individual academic satraps and concerns. All deal with questions as big as life and show a concern and a passion which speak for the enormous and only too rarely tapped energies which still lie largely submerged on our campuses. We will not all agree with their particular visions, but they say what they say in the service of a greater diversity to which we often pay homage, but to which too few are committed with what we nowadays call one's "gut."

One of the more remarkable aspects of *Change* Magazine is not that it makes possible civilized discourse among academic thought leaders, but that it is almost always concerned with remembering the human questions. Education, when worthy of the term, is an intensely human experience. These essays attest to this affirmation of the human possibility to persist against often very large odds. They mark but one small step in the direction of a new freedom, in which education deals with life and not with antiquities.

March 1972

The Education of Kate Haracz

JOURNAL OF AN UNDERGRADUATE

By Kate Haracz

FEBRUARY 2

It's still being Michigan outside— the mercury in all the thermometers hid. I headed all the way across campus in the sleet for my 12:40, and after twenty minutes I just wanted to bag it and crawl back into bed. (Why, oh *why* did I go to a school where some buildings are over a mile apart?) I tromped up the stairs into Social Stratification and found out that M., the prof, hadn't shown—he was sick, poor baby. That really ticked me off; you'd think that with all the facilities on this campus, they could notify students if a class were to be cancelled; WMSN could broadcast every hour on the hour. It would save a lot of grief.

M. didn't even bother showing until the third week of classes (and I've got two courses from him), and then when he did, I wished he hadn't bothered. He's one of the New Profs, the ones who come on casual and try to play it cool, knock the System, and in other ways try to con us into thinking that they're one of us, the great unwashed disaffected student body. I've had about four profs like that this year and they just turn me off—you can see the great big H for Hypocrite branded on their foreheads. They talk a great game, all right: I've heard the

spiels about "You're all getting screwed by the
university," "This classroom situation isn't meaningful" (that's a big word now, *meaningful*) and, best
of all, "Grades don't measure what you really learn."
And then they go right ahead and hand them out.
If they really believed that grades don't measure
learning, they should hand out blanket 4.0's; that
would be the quickest way to get rid of them—
how can you curve when everyone's at one end?
But they don't, and you know why? Because they've
got no guts. Last year, a prof tried blanket 4.0's
here and got canned for it. So profs like M. and
S. and G. and L., who all like their nice houses and
cool cars and private schools for their kids, duti-
fully distribute student numbers along a normal
curve and hand the results in to the registrar the
Monday after finals. They make me sick. I'd rather
have an old-school prof who laid it on the line, even
if I disagreed with him in principle, than one of
these guys who don't have the courage—or, more
important, the self-respect—to back up their smooth
speeches with action.

Funny thing, these are the very people who talk
about the tragedy of People Who Are Trapped by
the Materialistic American System. I wonder if they
ever look at themselves and see that they are just
as much a part of the system, just as much a part
of the tragedy as the people they put down. In fact,
I think they're more tragic, because they delude
themselves into thinking they're free when they're
not; at least some of the people in the system know
where they are, and they either accept it or work
to get out. These professors pride themselves on
being "liberated." You poor fools: open your eyes
and admit your chains are there. (The radio is now
beating out "Thank You for Lettin' Me Be Myself."
They should make it required listening for the New
Breed.)

FEBRUARY 3

I am hostile as hell right now—I've got the weekly Staff Meeting Blues. I hate staff meetings (for dorm Resident Advisors—RA's), first because they're meetings, which I detest in principle because they're circuitous, classic studies in communication breakdowns, and crashingly pompous and boring. (What is it about the mere fact of sitting at a table with X number of people that brings out the desire to impress, to conquer? Is it merely a ritualization of what we all do every day, only with gavels and motions instead of glances and cutting remarks? I don't care what they say about Michigan State being a Big Time, Big Ten football school—the real game here is meetings, and what goes on in conference rooms is more brutal, more violent, more damaging to people than anything that happens in Spartan Stadium.) I also hate these meetings because not only are we supposed to get all the bureaucratic junk from RHPO (Residence Halls Programs Office) and the Head Advisor, but we're also supposed to be dealing with each other on the staff as people, people with problems in being RA's, and we don't.

It isn't easy being an RA. (Some mornings I hum the chorus of the Ballad of John and Yoko as I brush my teeth.) A lot of times it's frustrating, so frustrating that half the girls' staff are working on ulcers. (We've named all the pains: there's Spearman, Heartburn Harry, Arnold the Ache, and we can rattle off the drugs from probanthine-15 to librax like we're pre-med students.) With forty-two girls, there just isn't enough time, and there isn't enough me to do all I want to. My floor is young (mostly freshmen and sophomores), and it's just beautiful to watch them grow; I cheer when I hear a kid say she's sorry but her parents don't know everything in the world, and it's time she told them that she's running her own life, or when a girl says she's going to sleep with a guy, or not sleep with him, because she's thought it over, and it's the right thing for her to do. It's wonderful to watch them think and experiment and learn who they are as people, as unique individuals who are good simply by being themselves.

But growing means pain, and that's when it starts getting rough for the RA. Or at least for me, and for most of the RA's in Case. That's because we view ourselves as friends and not the local law enforcement agency; all friends hurt when their friends do. I feel so helpless sometimes. I know I can't live other people's lives for them (I've enough trouble just ad-libbing my way through mine), they've got to make mistakes, they've got to get hurt if they're going to grow; but every time I see that veil in the eyes which tries but doesn't quite cover the hurt inside, something wrenches inside me. Twenty-four hours divided by forty-two girls just isn't enough time. So my stomach hurts, and I smoke a pack and a half a day, and I average four hours of sleep a night; but I'll get a note on my door or a get well card, or watch the antics in the hall, and that's enough. They're worth it. (Besides I can't be down today—the sun came out.)

FEBRUARY 4

Today was one of those supercold, icy Michigan days when nothing much happens, except that you discover that if you stand in the wind too long and you're wearing baggy bells, they're cold to sit on when the cattle car—the bus—finally comes. My stratification class hit a new low in boredom today: M. didn't have his stuff down and fumbled his way through an explanation of Marx on surplus value. I *really* would have been ticked at listening to something I got in high school, except that he was putting me to sleep (I read the desk graffiti and the signs on the bulletin boards to keep awake). Students really *are* idealists: I've had half a quarter from M. and should know by this time he's not going to say anything exciting or meaningful, and I should just stay home, but I keep hoping. So when I go I take a book, the Sunday *Times* crossword puzzle (at least I'm improving my vocabulary), and count the minutes until he stops. It's sad when I contrast this course with another I've got on political philosophy. The prof there is much the same type as M.—the young, cool ones—but he's much more self-assured, has the material down cold, and is a natural comic. The class is relaxed, hisses when he mentions the midterm, and goes off on great tangents. I like it even though I'm not outstandingly good at piecing together philosophical arguments.

While flipping through this morning's *State News* (the daily blatz—we call it the *Stale News*—which greets us every morn with nothing more readable than Peanuts), I saw an ad for Inland Steel which really made me sad. It said "College is a waste of time . . . unless you get a good job afterwards." I think maybe I slept through part of the standard American socialization process, because somehow I missed the lesson on College as Vocational Training. I know very well there's nothing I can do with a degree from an experimental social sciences college except go to grad school, but I don't really care, I've enjoyed (hear that, M.?—*enjoyed*) just messing around with different kinds of knowledge and seeing new things, new relationships that I never knew existed. I like picking up bits and pieces all over this university (I think they call it Exploring Your Interests in the better educational circles) because I'm interested in just about everything. The whole crazy world is a circus and I'm not going to waste my front row seat by carefully studying the drift patterns of the sawdust on the floor. *Hey, all*

*you out there at Inland Steel: Did you ever read any-
thing that didn't have to do with the sacred rituals
that go on in that American place of worship, the
Office? Did you ever read Toynbee or Kennan or
Brunner or Hesse or (shock) science fiction? Cereal
boxes? Anything at all, just because it was interesting or different or because you were curious or just
for the hell of it?* I'm beginning to think living is a
waste of time if you do get a good job after college.
And the saddest part about it is that many kids in
school now believe Inland Steel. *Don't worry,
America, you'll get your career-oriented engineers
and advertising experts because not everyone was
lucky enough to fall asleep during the lecture on
College as Vocational Training, and they will graduate, right on schedule, with a brain that's 2 percent
hypertrophied and the rest dead, with personalities
that will meld nicely with The Way Things Are, and
they'll never know the fun they're missing.* That's
right, fun. Idealist that I am, even two years at a
multiversity have not convinced me that learning
can't be something I like doing. Or that there aren't
profs around who like teaching. I guess I'm an in-
curable case. One thing I have learned for certain,
in a world where most of what you learn consists
of learning that what you learned before isn't so, is
that I'm going to give my kids Sominex when the
lecture on college comes on.

The Funny Things that Go On in a Dorm Department: Janie just knocked at my door and said,
"Jersey, come here quick." As I made my way out
the door, I looked up and saw a guy braced between
the two walls of the hall, nine feet up. He slid down
one wall and said, "Hi." I said, "Great." It really
thrills me to know that the people around here have
refused to be impressed with the sanctity of the dorm
and use it as it's meant to be—as a toy.

FEBRUARY 8

The typical Sunday, but sans *New York Times*
(one must make some concession to midterms).
Slept late, rejected what Case cafeteria was passing
off as food, booked (Thomas Hobbes is finally starting to make sense; seeing as I've got the mid
tomorrow, it's really convenient), and played bridge.

I really miss Tommy. It's so hard to think of
his being 11,000 miles away. The thing I hate
most is not knowing if he's all right. It only takes
three seconds to die, but it will take the Army a
week to notify me. He could be dead right now,
as I think of his green eyes and curly brown hair,
and I wouldn't know. The silence is what gets me,
the sending letters into a void, not knowing if he'll
ever read them, or if I'll ever get an answer, the
looking at my ring and wondering if I'll ever get
the matching wedding band, the planning of a future
while making sure there are alternate plans. If he
should be killed, I'd be as close to being destroyed
as I can imagine being, but more than that, I'd feel
robbed. I know what I want to do with my life—
marry Tommy and have his children—and if they
kill him, they've taken away my future. Old men
should fight the battles—they're the ones who start
them; and more than that, they've lived, they've
made their choices—most important, they've had

the chance to choose. It's not right that they should take my chance away from me; the war started before I was born, before Tommy was born, before my parents had met. It's not my war, I don't support it—why should I have to pay, why should I have to stare at the walls of a dorm room and wonder what a jungle looks like, wonder about death and try to accept the fact that it means gone forever, not just three months or a year or ten years but *forever*, with no appeal? Why should I suffer because some old fat men in Washington decide that some spot on the map is worth killing hundreds of thousands of people for when I can't even vote to throw them out? Someone has said that the quickest way to end war is to make the "statesmen" fight it, and they're right. "Come ye masters of war, ye who lie and deceive, a world war can be won, you want me to believe. . . ." *Yes, come on, Dickie and Lyndon and John and Ike, come fight on the front lines, come lug a gun, come be a target for* VC *basic training. You keep talking about "commitment"—well, I measure commitment by how much a person puts out on his own. You believe that Nam is vitally important? Well, do something—enlist. Put your life on the line in this cruddy war, not someone else's, not someone else who doesn't believe in what you're doing but figures he'd better go and be a medic and pick up the pieces of what's left. No, huh? You're all a bunch of hypocrites who talk a good game and cop out when the important things, like your own lives, are on the line.*

Two weeks from today is my birthday, and I'll be twenty-one. I'll try the ballot box first, just to say I've tried it. (My Soc and Poli Sci courses have taught me that one vote does nothing against the moneyed interests. But, America, what are you going to do when the 50 percent of the 18-22 popu-

lation which is now in college gets a little bit older
and starts moving into society? Did you ever consider the fact that mass higher education may be
the death of your nicely organized society?) And
then I'll move out, into the streets, because I believe in backing up my beliefs with action. (Just
wait. Your time is gonna come.)

Well, kiddies, it's midterm time. Batten down FEBRUARY 9
the hatches and shift into overdrive, because that's
the only way you're going to survive. Tonight a
lot of my frosh are uptight because the ones in
Madison have their Policy Problems mid tomorrow;
so I filled a couple of mugs with candy and went on
a door-to-door study break, and happily blew the
evening talking to people (what the hell, my next
mid isn't until day after tomorrow).

I am really going through some changes as a
person this year. I'm beginning to discover that
even though I knew objectively that my parents
were often wrong in the way they raised me, I
still believed and acted upon the things they taught
me when I was young, like feeling that I must
always be proving myself, and that no matter what
I do it's not quite good enough.

Well, today was Monday, and that meant another session with my counselor. I think going to
see one was the smartest thing I ever did, because
even though it was against all my standards to admit
that everything wasn't going all right, and that
maybe I needed some help to talk things through,
and it hurt to admit I couldn't cope with it all by
myself (like I spent twenty years doing), I found
that it helps me to see myself in a different light,
which for me means as a somewhat better person.
I know some beautiful people, some people who
really care about other people, who are open and

just wonderful to be with. You know the one thing they have in common? They all think they're basically worthless, or not good enough, and it's just not true. They're *great* people—what happened to them, what did their parents do to make them feel worthless? What did the Spock method do to turn out such good people who think that they're worthless? Anyway, to get back to the counselor: It was quite a session, because I keep getting closer to the things I know are wrong but can't admit are wrong, because if they're gone, if all the things I learned aren't true, what's left? It's frightening. My counselor keeps telling me that *I'm* left, that I'm a good person; but I can't believe it, not yet. Maybe someday I'll believe that I'm worth something, that people can like me for me, even with everything that's wrong with me, but not yet. It takes a while, I've found, to unlearn twenty years.

M an, a really classic case of generation gap FEBRUARY 11 tonight: Cathy and I were interviewing three RA candidates, and we went bopping out to the Hospitality Inn's coffee shoppe (that extra *pe* is for extra class). We'd been there about two hours and had almost finished the interviews (as well as our food; the poor waitress was dismayed when I ordered pecan pancakes, a chocolate shake and onion rings—I'm sorry but dinner in the dorm really lost tonight: we played name it and claim it—and she's lucky I didn't order a pistachio shake and chili like I usually do) when the father figure walks in, plops his bod down next to us, and announces that he's all for us doing our own bag *(doing our own bag?* Well, that's what he said), and all parents want is for their children to be happy. Aha, I thought, an enlightened adult. *Wrong, Katie, wrong.*

This guy was almost the compleat adult which we kids have come to know and despise (not despise really, just want to avoid at all costs). His major hang up was sex; the conversation (monologue, actually) oscillated between tirades against "cheapie girls" and "I could lay you tomorrow." (We all sat there, repulsed at the thought.) Next, he came out with "America is the best country on earth." (Did you know that the Constitution, Bill of Rights and Declaration of Independence contain the sacred justification for the American business system? Neither did I, but being the respectful, well-brought-up child that I am, I listened to and heeded my elder's words of wisdom.) "And we've left it to you kids, and you're going to give it all away with your pot and free love and wake up and find the communists ruling and, boy, then won't you be sorry." (We tried to point out that while we agreed with American democratic principles, we'd just like to see them practiced for a change. No soap.) And then came the final, incredible statement that "everything we did was right at the time." Now, I'm not one to categorically knock people of my father's generation; I think that the majority of them did what they thought was right at the time, but there's a big difference between what you *think* is right, and what turns out to be the best thing. It's just a minor human failing which we're all, even my father's generation, even or especially my generation, subject to. He started on the "youth today has too much money" bit, but dropped it when we nailed him with, "Who gave it to us?" Then, as we left, he said he hoped we would all marry Republicans. Marry a Republican? *Yecch.*

It's really sad. He's so lonely and unsure, and can't understand why his children have rejected him. And the saddest thing of all is that there are so many insecure, uptight parents like him in this country, parents who fought so hard for what the System told them was good; and the Depression created such an intense desire to possess material goods that they've forgotten there are other values in life. It's always what you don't have as a kid that's important when you're an adult. They had families but no money, so they want a Better Homes and Gardens house; we had Better Homes and Gardens houses and wanted a family and love. I can understand how my father's generation got the way it is, why material things are so important—I'd probably have ended up the same way. I just wish they'd step into my life for a while and see what I didn't have, and why I want the things I do. My father belongs to the last of the generations to believe in the Great American Promise that material goods shall make you happy, while I belong to the first of the generations which has discovered that not only do material goods not bring heaven on earth, they can turn it into an absolute hell. They found the answers to life in the traditional American ideals—all they needed was the money; we've got the money, and found out that the old ideals aren't worth having anymore.

I   FEBRUARY 12
can find the funniest things to get depressed about. Today I sold The Folly, my truck, because I can't afford it any more. I really hate to see it go—I spent the two best summers of my life in it. The memories: Tommy and I camping out at Crystal Lake (and the most fantastic view of the stars I've ever seen); Nell and I camping out in the Brookchester Apartments parking lot because we had no place else to stay; that fantastic trip to St. Louis with Kelly, Mike, Dave and Terry (sixteen hours, two flats and a busted heater); the blowouts, the one fifty miles south of Dallas where two twin

girls who had just gotten married in a double cere-
mony at seven that night and their new husbands
took me to the nearest station, twenty miles away,
and the one on the Natchez Trace in Mississippi,
the most scenic place to have a blowout that I know
of; driving through Missouri in a tornado; the South,
from Jackson to Fayetteville, nonstop, alone and
at night; the Finger Lakes of Upstate New York.
Requiem for a truck: 25,000 miles in fifteen
months, and the best times of my life.

So for therapy I rearranged my room. For two
and a half years I've always operated on the theory
that a room should be functional. Well, that theory
died tonight—I've got my desk tucked in a corner
(you have to trip over the bookcase holding this
term's texts to get at it), the back seat of my
truck is under the window, making it impossible
to make the bed, and my two and a half foot tall
liquor bottle lamp is in front of the door to the
study lounge. I wasn't feeling particularly functional
or rational tonight; I also didn't realize how many
books I had—I started counting, got through one
shelf and had seventy-eight, and chickened out and
stopped. Must be over $1,000 in books here, and
that's only since I graduated from high school.
I can see myself at seventy-three in an eighteen-room
mansion which houses my books and nothing else.
(Tommy's just as bad; our first apartment will be
Neo-Orange Crate and Early Paperback.)

Took a mindblow of a mid today. The test itself wasn't bad, it was the concept of the test that
zapped me out. The course is Small Group Interaction, which would lead one to think in terms of
many, many nuances of behavior, subtleties which
could only be hinted at, even on an essay test. Get
this: true-false. TRUE-FALSE. I somehow feel that
a true-false test just doesn't measure adequately
one's knowledge of what people do. (My God,

could you see what would happen if everyone started thinking of other people in true-false terms? *Jane is a nice girl—true or false?)* Besides, I'm ticked because this test reflects the prof's attitude toward the entire course ("Now Homans's first proposition is. . . ."); besides, 1 can't stand lazy profs—and he's got lecture notes dated 1955; besides, why should I spend my time going to class when I can read the book? Why bother?

FEBRUARY 13

One of those blah Michigan winter days when nothing much happens and nobody cares: even the TG's (Friday afternoon beer blasts) were few and far between. A lot of people went home this weekend, because most mids are over; Case is a ghost town.

Got a letter from Tommy and discovered that where he's been assigned isn't even on my map; all I know is that it's near the Cambodian border where all the fighting's going on. "Light another cigarette, learn to forget, learn to forget. . . ."

The second batch of ADS kids showed up today. I really sympathized with one guy from West Orange, N.J., who was on his first trip to Michigan; the look in his eyes said, "Get me out of this strange place where there's nothing for miles but snow." That was exactly the way I felt when I came here —it's like another planet. Just the thought of being 780 miles away from home is frightening, especially to an Easterner who's used to thinking of trips to Philly and D.C. as major excursions. That's one thing I've discovered: the further West you go, the shorter long distances seem. When I was a. freshman, I had a roommate from Idaho who blew my mind by telling me she lived 13½ hours from the state u. and kids drove home for the weekend.

There's just no way to express how alien I sometimes feel in Michigan or other parts of the country, how totally incomprehensible the way some of my friends grew up seems to me. Like Dave—his town had 3,000 people in it; or Terry, who comes from Mississippi, where just about everything is different from New York. I'm glad I came out here to school, because a kid who's spent all her life within thirty miles of New York City needs to know there are other ways of thinking and feeling and acting besides those you get over WNBC, and traveling through eighteen states a summer has taught me the only geography I know, but I really get homesick for New York sometimes. I like that rush and constant excitement; I know who I am, and being alone in the middle of eight million people doesn't make me feel lost, like it does some of my friends who visit there—I'm me and the impersonality of New York can't take that away from me, and I like having to choose between things I want to do, rather than what I'll settle for, like I do here. Most of all, it's home; I'm a city person at heart, and I always will be. I love the freedom I find there; it's my turf, despite all the things that are wrong with it, and I love it: it's me.

Mom and Sheila came up and dropped Sue   FEBRUARY 14
off (she'll stay until Tuesday afternoon; she doesn't have school because of a teachers' conference).

It always messes me up to see them all, because I can't give them what they demand. I carefully disassociated myself from my family when the divorce occurred (I had to maintain my sanity—it's no fun watching the hostilities), but I've always wanted to be able to like and love and just have a family. And I can't. I can't love them, there are days when I can't even like them, and yet, somehow, someway, I want to. I don't like the ambiguity; it would be so much easier if I could love them and respect them, or if I could just cut all the strings. At one point, I thought I had it good— I was the only kid I knew who didn't have to fight her way out of the house; my house moved out from under me. They've been treating me as an adult lately, or at least as more of one, but I think I'm going to have to go away for a few years and then come back before they'll really treat me as a real live grown-up. And by then I'll not feel bad about being me, about living the way I want to.

The thing I want most is not to be treated as a prize poodle. They wanted me to perform, to bring home the grades, to be a model daughter— without any problems. It's not going to happen to my kids: my kids are going to be *kids*. My kids are going to be told that it's all right to be sloppy and lazy and angry if that's what they feel like, and they're going to be told that I'll still love them, and that by being sloppy or lazy or angry they won't risk losing my love, because I'm going to let them be *all* of themselves, not just the socially acceptable parts. They're going to have a childhood, and not just a period of their life which is a miniature adulthood; I'm not going to ask a little kid to act like an adult, or to feel like an adult, or to take on the responsibilities of an adult, because he's not one, and nobody's got any right to expect him to behave with the veneer of an adult. Besides, I don't want my kids to be like most of the adults I know—like that guy in the Hospitality Inn. Forget it, baby, you can just bag it, because I'm not buying it—not for my kids, not for me.

M onday—M.'s travesty. He keeps talking about how the technology of the kindergarten and   FEBRUARY 16 the technology of the college classroom are essentially the same. It's a decent point, but he ruins it, so I brought a coloring book and crayons.

Another travesty: the contempt sentences of the Chicago Eight or Seven or Nine or Ten, depending on how you keep score. When Jerry Rubin spoke here in January, he said their main purpose was to show the farce of the American judicial system. They couldn't have succeeded better, and it achieved another goal—it radicalized, to a greater or lesser degree, many people like myself who, while they agreed with some of their objectives, disagreed with or even opposed their tactics. I don't see how anybody can agree with the old notion of free trials by peers any longer—it was trial by judge, pure and simple. One of my friends said, "It's not a farce any longer—it's downright dangerous." Couldn't the government have found anybody, like *any body,* one off the street even, to conduct a trial which at least looked fair? (At one time I thought I was a liberal middle-of-the-roader; now I find myself still believing in many of the same things but being pushed left by the actions of people like Johnson and Nixon, who are somehow defined as the American political mainstream.) And I wonder what a lot of blacks think about the fact that a lawyer was sentenced to over a year in jail for embracing Ralph Abernathy.

FEBRUARY 18

In the mailbox this morning: a tape from Tommy. It racked me up. I'm glad to hear from him, and to hear his voice again, but it was so strange. At times, it didn't sound like him—the sound of his voice was different.

I've developed ways of not thinking of it, of not feeling the hurt, but today it was back in full force: the defenses weren't made to handle tapes, I guess.

Tommy said he found two little children who had
been playing with a detonator which exploded and
burned them badly; Tommy and the guys he was
with picked up the kids and took them to a hospital.
Tommy said the worst thing he had ever experienced
was riding in the jeep with a little boy screaming in
agony on his lap, and not being able to do anything
for him; I could hear it in his voice. What a rotten
war. Then the tape ran out in the middle of a
mortar attack.

(As I'm writing this, I'm getting all sorts of hassle from Annette, who says I editorialize with my
face, and that it's the funniest thing she's seen since
a year ago Shrove Tuesday. It's very hard to type
when someone's cracking up at you.)

Cut my afternoon classes—I've reached the
conclusion that I can put my time to better use by
staying home and reading the stuff than I can by
going to class. Which is really bad. Says something
about the non-education I'm getting. I stayed home
and read two books and slept for four hours.
Finished *Steppenwolf:* I agreed with some of Hesse's
premises, like the essential fluidity of one's personality, and that one has more power in shaping one's
life and personality than we're usually led to believe, but what he did with it—the killing of Her-
mine, especially—did not seem to be an affirmation
of this, and Haller, even after he was sentenced to
life, didn't really seem to get the point.

It was a good study of guilt complexes, and
the desire for punishment which so many people
have had drummed into them; I can understand
now why college kids like it, because what our
parents tried to do was make us feel guilty. "If
you do that, Mommy (will be disappointed) (will
be hurt) (won't love you anymore)." And a lot
of us are just waking up to this fact, and have taken
a look at ourselves, and we are finding out we're

much better people than our parents led us to believe, and won't stand for the old guilt games. Essentially, it's a rejection of our parents' definition of what constitutes a good, valuable person, and this fact is going to have to be realized by our parents.

FEBRUARY 19

Gleefully cut M.'s 8:00. It was Glenn's turn to go (we play cooperate and graduate). Got up relatively early and booked and did shitwork for the Small Group class, which was its usual abysmal self. Booked and slept all afternoon and evening, talked to people—the usual stuff.

There was a rally up at the Union tonight to protest the conspiracy trial verdict. I heard from friends who were there that cops were crawling all over the place, and that things even got as far as car-rocking (radicalism hits a new high at State). The news on the radio just said they arrested kids, that there were about two dozen injuries, and that windows were smashed in some stores. This could actually develop into something, but I doubt it. First, nobody knows who's behind tonight's rally, and second, when I talked to kids who were going, they were all out for blood. I can't tolerate that, and I think it reveals some serious inconsistencies in the thinking of the rally leaders, who theoretically abhor the senseless violence of Vietnam. I am not against the use of violence as a revolutionary means —I've just got to be damn sure that it's the only way out.

At one point, I was something of a pacifist, but not anymore, not since I learned that there are other ways to kill people besides stopping their bodily functions; I think it's worse to mangle a person's mind than his body, because at least a dead person doesn't feel it anymore. I can honestly now see myself, at some point, under certain conditions, using violence. I wouldn't have said that two years ago. I'm still thinking it through, and I'll probably work through the System first, but if that doesn't work, I'm not going to sit by and watch it ruin my life and those of millions of other people. What has not yet emerged is a serious revolutionary movement which is dedicated to revolution and not intra-party politics, which plans for results and not effect. That's when Spiro & Friends should start to worry, because it'll mean that the youth movement has finally gotten down to business.

While I'm writing this, all the normal things are happening in my room: Annette is maligning me and cracking up at the faces I'm making, there have been three people in here generally breaking each other up, a five-minute bad pun session with Terry, the Firesign Theater is blaring out of the radio, two phone calls, and there's the usual noise from kids in the hall. The Circus, one of the unofficial names for my floor, rolls on. I don't think I could stand a superstraight book-it floor—it would drive me up a wall. My kids are all eccentric, and I love their spontaneity, even when I feel like I'm living in a world that's a cross between the French surrealist directors of the twenties and *Mad* magazine. Besides, I'm just as bad.

FEBRUARY 20

Today's major accomplishments were blowing this month's clothes budget on stuff to wear to work this summer and listening to records all night. (I don't like soul at all—give me acid rock.)

After last night's fracas, the campus was incredibly quiet—you'd think nothing had happened —no tension or anything. It is almost impossible to launch any sustained campus uprising during a Michigan winter (today's high was seventeen—not too many people are going to march in that). Spring term, however, is another story, because after a Michigan winter, everybody and his mother's maiden aunt are ready to tear this place down, just to work off excess energy.

We should have some drug busts this spring, because it's an election year. (It's really fun living four miles down the road from the state capital; one incredible senator actually got upset because he'd heard that boys and girls were "eating pizza together in the dorms at ten and eleven o'clock at night.") And the busts will be held during finals week because the *State News* doesn't publish then, and the students don't have sufficient information to launch demonstrations. (Much as I dislike this, it's comforting to know that something in this world is predictable.)

FEBRUARY 21

Normally when I sit down to the typewriter it's after midnight and technically no longer the day which appears at the top of the page. However, since I have now operationally defined morning as that time of day when I get up, even if it's 3 P.M., and the end of the day as that time of day when I go to bed, even if it's 8 A.M., this doesn't bother me; in fact, since I've become a big fan of the afternoon nap, some days have two mornings. Today, there is a new and exciting innovation—it's only 10:30 P.M. Actually, there's an ulterior motive: I turn twenty-one at midnight and I'm going to hit the Gables, and when I finally make it back, I don't think I'll have any inclination to write.

This is a strange birthday, for several reasons. First (and most important) is the fact that Tommy isn't around, like he has been for the last three. Then, I'm at that point in life where I change from being a Minor in Possession to Contributing to the Delinquency of Minors. But since I've already turned legal once (in New York City when I was eighteen), it doesn't have quite the thrill it did before.

I guess another reason is that turning twenty-one, becoming an adult legally, doesn't really mean anything. It's funny, because last year, before I turned twenty, I felt so horribly old because I wasn't going to be a teen-ager anymore—it really shook me up, because I'd spent a third of my life being one and had gotten used to thinking of myself as one (it's called identity crisis in *In* circles). This year I could really care less about the legal definitions because I know that twenty-one years of existence don't guarantee maturity, that maturity is a continuing process, and that when I'm forty I'll still have growing to do. Besides, it's always been harder for me to leave something (possibly because for so much of my life things and people and relationships have been leaving me and because no sooner had I gotten things straightened out again than everything would change again) than to face something new, since I've got almost unlimited confidence in my ability to bluff my way through anything. And anyway, adulthood has never impressed me much; I've spent a lot of time looking at adults and I don't think too much of a lot of them, or the way they act. I find that I like people because I like them as *people,* and that age is not a major criterion for being a good person.

So much for adulthood—I've got to get dressed so I can do the town (what there is of it). The campus is bigger than East Lansing.

FEBRUARY 22

What an absolutely fine birthday—just stellar. Of course, the first bar Doug and I went to wouldn't serve me because of some strange Michigan law about a bar's day being from opening until closing, and consequently it was still considered the twenty-first (even though it was past midnight), and the second bar was parked out to Detroit (I wondered if they were shipping people into other dimensions, because there was no way that the people who came out of all those cars could fit into a place that size). But we finally made it to the Gables, where I got the free champagne and beer, and had a really great time at the Show Bar (which is a large, rolling party). Then followed one of the funniest bridge games I've ever played.

When I woke up at eleven, Terry, Annette and Gloria kept hassling me about being aged. Then the Let's Freak Out Mommy and Daddy started. The phone rang, and Terry picked it up with "Home for the Aged"—and of course my mother thought she had the wrong number.

Then, I was innocently sitting next door when about twenty people walked in, dragged me into my room, and proceeded to toilet paper both me and it in pink paisley TP. What a shambles—at one point I was toilet papered into my room, because they were using me as a post to anchor the stuff on. Then I was moved down to Bailey's apartment on the third floor, where they had German chocolate cake (Annette is such a fine cook), and they proceeded to give me my birthday present: a do-it-yourself wig kit. Everyone had contributed a lock of hair. It's really classy. Actually, it was symbolic of the collection they took up so that I could buy a short, curly stretch wig (which I've coveted for a long time). It's not that I don't like long, straight black hair—it's just that after three years of it, a temporary change every now and then will be nice.

Terry pushed me into my room, the phone rang, Chris answered, "Office of Student Affairs—do you want one?" and turned six shades of purple when I said, "Hi, Dad." We went out to the House of Pancakes, and I got my twenty-one free pancakes (which I gave to Kelly); and we went to the Fifth Dimension concert. Now, "Up, Up and Away" etc. is not really my kind of music, but it was a fitting end to a marvelous day. For a birthday which I expected to be a real downer, it turned out to be one of the better ones I've had. My friends are such wonderful people.

A FEBRUARY 23
nother wipe-out day. It started when I went over to pre-enroll, and found out that the university has dropped two courses—eight credits—which I had planned to take spring term. I was really ticked.

Then I finished one of M.'s midterms (done at 10:10, due at 12:40) and started his other mid (due tomorrow). Actually, I'm glad he gave the take-homes—it's the only way I'm learning anything out of either of his courses; I certainly don't get anything out of his lectures. I am disgusted with my "education" this term; I can't understand how I could enjoy things so much last term and have them go so completely sour this term. (Last term was unique: it was the only term I've actually enjoyed every one of my courses.)

The *Stale News* came out with editorial comments against last Thursday's fracas. I generally agreed, because their main point was not anti-violence, but the fact that Thursday's violence was senseless and irrelevant. Smashing windows at Jacobsen's has little to do with the conspiracy trial; I wish the fools who did it would realize that all they did was add another black mark on the youth movement score sheet. Idiots.

I'm in a bind, because essentially I agree with most of what the New Left says, but I cannot go along with what I consider to be senseless methods of attempting to achieve change. So I don't march (at least not often), and I don't throw bricks at department store windows. (The stores raised their already exorbitant prices today—the kids only hurt themselves.) But I find that there is little I can accept about American society today, and even that is rapidly decreasing, and there is, at the moment, no way in which I can express my opinions.

Received a card from Tommy today which read: FEBRUARY 25 "Sorry for lack of mail. Won't be able to write for the next month. Please don't worry. I'll explain later." Well, we all know what that means—patrol time. And back to not knowing, to checking the *Times* for the casualty lists every Wednesday and Saturday, to sending letters off into the void. It hurts so far down that I'm numb.

M.'s class again: today, as he sauntered into the room, you could tell he'd made up his mind to be cool. He sat in the back of the room and waited. About twenty minutes after the class was supposed to start, he said, "What do you want to do today?" (I thought of several unrepeatable suggestions, and one or two illegal ones.) Of course, two kids immediately took over the class and started talking about advertising and management, which nobody wanted to listen to. *Question: Who put you up there in the first place? Answer: Abdication of a non-teacher.*

It soon degenerated into another session of liberal breast-beating about values in education and how rotten the System is. I walked out. I've got better things to do than listen to this crap which they all take so seriously like they have just discovered the secret of the universe. They actually think it daring (and consequently cool) to say that the System reeks. Yippityshit. I'm sick of all the tearful, Monday-morning, gutless-wonder soul-searching. When are they going to realize the American system is oppressive, irrelevant to the needs of the modern world, and a stacked deck besides? Democracy is fine by me—let's have a free, open society, instead of what we've got now. "If you'd just use the proper channels everything would work out fine," say all the New Deal liberals. Well, they don't realize (or perhaps they do) that the channels are not avenues of access to the decision-making process, but means of channeling behavior into safe paths, paths that won't rock the boat. Channels are supposed to be the way the People exercise their voice in a democracy; but those in power define the channels, and thereby limit the People's voice. When are people going to open their eyes and see? When are they going to look at what really happens, instead of what they would like to think happens? (I saw a movie on the Chicago convention today, and all that a lot of the people interviewed kept saying was, "I can't believe it—it can't happen here." Well, baby, it can, and did, and does.)

FEBRUARY 26

It hurts me to see other people hurt, especially when they're such good people and are trying so hard to get their heads on straight. It's so easy to hand out the old line about never changing or growing without pain, but it's a different story when you see the pain in a girl's eyes as she says, "I'm really trying, and I don't mean to come across the way I do—I didn't even know I came across that way." And being honest with each other is such a dangerous thing, because sometimes "Let's be honest" really means "Now's my chance to say what I've been wanting to say to you all along— I hate your guts, chick." No wonder so few people trust each other; it's so sad that when we let go

of our polite veneer, there's so much hate to get
rid of before the good parts of people can come
out. That's probably why all my friends think
they're no good—all they've been taught is to
repress the hate, and they learn to hate the hate,
and themselves for hating; all they see is the hate,
because they've never been taught to look for anything else. We were never taught that it's all right
to hate, because it's part of us, and we *are* valuable,
even when we're not particularly nice. Our parents
neatly compartmentalized our selves, and accepted
only the nice parts; they never realized that by
bottling up the hate, they bottled up the love, because if you've been conditioned never to show
your emotions as strongly as they really exist, when
the time comes that you want to show a strong
emotion, you can't, at least not openly and freely,
only for itself and with no games thrown in. Why
did they think we were wild animals to be tamed?
Why didn't they see us as beautiful people to be
helped to grow and develop?

I think the thing I want most to do is to get rid
of my superego. (Did you ever think to connect
increasing suicide rates among young people and
greater frequency of ulcers and other nervous problems with the permissive theory of child-raising?
Permissive, hell. It's sadistic: a spanking is nothing
compared to the terrors a four-year-old can have
if he thinks Mommy will leave him if he's not a
good boy.) I want to get rid of the notion that I
must constantly prove myself to be loved; I want
to be loved for just being me, for just being.
Instead, I'm stuck with all the screwy ideas about
personal value that got programmed into me when
I was too young to know better.

I look at people, like that salesman at the
Hospitality Inn, and see all the pain they lug around
inside them, and the little cages they're locked up

in, and the hate they have for the cages, and the overwhelming fear they have that someone will take the cages away. They're like Marlowe's Mephistopheles: "Why, this is hell, nor am I out of it." And in a sense they hate us for ripping down our bars, for escaping the portable hell inside our skulls, because free and open people destroy the security of *their* uptight world by showing that their world is not the only one around, and by challenging them to rip down *their* bars; and that's where the whole generation gap lies: we think we can and so we try; they're afraid they can't and so they don't.

FEBRUARY 27

This is the stage of complete mental wipe-out. I have written three papers today (all one-copy specials, hot off the typewriter; after eight quarters here, I've gotten so much practice at them that they're usually as good as the ones I write out first, but thanks for eraseable paper). I am sitting here staring at the typewriter. It is definitely getting down to the wire—only two more weeks of class before finals—and it is an absolute necessity to start now if you're going to make it through. These papers I typed today, well, they're only three of the six I have to turn in the last two days of class; it's really a rotten system, because you have to spend all your time working on the papers the profs assign for the end of the term, and that leaves you with one weekend to book for finals, and if you have take-homes as well as in-class exams (like I do), you're up the creek. One week of spring break will definitely not be enough to recuperate.

There is never enough time to just relax and do nothing; the pressure is constantly on; there is always something you should be doing. I want time to be me, and without feeling I should really be

booking or writing a paper. A lot of profs still
have that great old notion that education is only
books, and that one should spend all one's time
developing one's mind, and they all hand out assignments like theirs was the only class in town.

Today's university is not geared for the total
person. You take neatly compartmentalized courses
in neat departments, you live in made-by-Nabisco
dorms, you do certain things at certain times (you
can't take a class at three A.M., even if you're the
sort of person who likes to sleep all day and wakes
up only in the small hours). And all those nice old
deans and profs wonder why students are upset.
I want to be me, and I want a place which will help
me to integrate my new experiences. Competency
in compartments isn't enough. I want the right to
be a total person.

FEBRUARY 28

Pete called tonight. Tommy is in a hospital in
Yokohama with second-degree burns over 50 percent of his body. It happened on my birthday. I
can't write anymore.

Black Literature, Relevance, and the New Irrationality

By Irvin Stock

I teach English at an American university, and nowadays—this has, of course, become a familiar plaint—the world I work in is growing increasingly irrational. And self-righteous about it, too, as if reasoning were for bad guys. Not from students alone, but from colleagues and their articles and books has been coming lately, under the guise of protest against social injustice, a stream of attacks on the human mind—on its freedom, its variousness, its complexity. In a number of highfalutin ways, we are being told that the intellectual life is a battle of self-interest (or class interest or race interest), in which art, reason, principles, intellectual techniques and safeguards are mere rationalizations for the brute inner grunt which means "I want it so" or "I don't want it so," and men can hope to communicate only with those who are already grunting in unison with them.

Now to anyone who remembers how, in certain quarters, Stalinism degraded the intellectual life of the thirties such notions—and the answer they require—are not new. Still, here they are again, and again they have to be answered. Not only does a generation exist for whom the thirties are dim, or romanticised ancient history. The view of mind they represent is perennially persuasive, like any half-truth that supports "good" against "evil." And it seems to me that the answer, as often in the past, must show both where they are false and where they are true.

The current attack on mind in the universities takes three main forms: the ethnic approach to literature, the demand for "relevance," and the denial of the possibility of objectivity. Here, to show exactly what has to be dealt with, are some examples of each.

A talented black novelist recently told me that our apparent communication was an illusion. The only reality in our relationship was that he was a victim of colonialism and I was a member of the class of colonialists. (He, my well-paid colleague, whose novels clearly belong to the Western tradition of realism; and I, the son of poor Jews who had fled their own oppressors and slaved to put me through college.) Then, the Afro-American Society of a university sent a memo to its English Department not long ago explaining that no white teacher should ever be permitted to teach black literature "because no person has the ability to stand outside his own conditioning." To communicate with black men at all, the white man must "recognize that he comes to black literature as an alien and ultimately as an enemy." (A black teacher of Shakespeare was alarmed by such "racism" into thoughts of leaving the university. It seemed to imply no Negro could teach Shakespeare.) This position is carried into esthetic theory by black Professor Addison Gayle, Jr. In his book *The Black Situation* we read, "Young black writers for whom the city is home ... accept the basic premises of Black Nationalism—that black people are different from other Americans—and ... that such differences mandate a differ-ent literature." Further: "The theory of the masterpiece," that is, the idea that literature has standards of excellence and truth not identical with its usefulness to any group "...was put forth by men who sought to erect a barrier between themselves and other men.... However, the black writer can never accept elitism, or a barrier which separates him from other black men.... He replaces the formula 'art for art's sake' ... with the humane formula 'art for the peoples' sake.' "

Nor do such notions come only from black national-
ists. The white critic Richard Gilman, in his book *The
Confusion of Realms,* declares that whites have no right to
judge books like Malcolm X's *Autobiography* or Cleaver's
Soul on Ice because "we whites . . . . are, vis-a-vis the
blacks, the imperialists. This is why our vocabularies of
rational discourse are so different from black Americans'
(when a subject people finds its voice at last, it has to be
different from its masters'). The old Mediterranean values—the belief in the sanctity of the individual soul, the
importance of logical clarity, brotherhood, reason as
arbiter, political order, community—are dead as *useful*
frames of reference or pertinent guides to procedure."

As for the current idea of "relevance," we are helped
to understand this by an article in *Change,* May-June, 1970,
by Professor Louis Kampf of M.I.T. Kampf says he felt
"uneasy" about his work on Pope when he realized that,
though himself "a socialist, I was taking a friend of [Tory]
Lord Bolingbroke as my model." After calling literature at
present "a weapon in the hands of imperialism" ("Whom
did the values represented by Homer's Achilles serve? . . . Is
the counterrevolutionary acceptance of fate in tragedy
something we are supposed to teach as a received value?"),
he tells us, with, I suppose, commendable candor, how
boring the "Western masterpieces" have become in his own
classes. His class in Proust, for instance, took on a little life
only after he had transferred it to the M.I.T. student center,
which had become a sanctuary for draft resisters. But not
enough life, apparently, for he ends the anecdote by
doubting that he will teach Proust again. Even more odd, he
reports that "after some months of unexciting classes" he
and his students woke up only when a young man in one
class, in order to make some personal contact with a group
of students who were shouting slogans, undressed and then
resumed his seat naked. General discussion continued until

"a female student shouted, 'Bullshit. There is a naked man
sitting next to me. We're all thinking of him, yet no one's
saying a word.' So for the next two hours we discussed why
he had taken off his clothes, and how that related to our
being in class and to the books we were reading. It was the
only lively discussion we had all semester." Of course, that
he has had some boring classes is not especially to his
discredit. What teacher hasn't? The significant thing is
where he places the blame.

And in *College English*, March, 1970, Stanford Professor Bruce Franklin goes a bit further. In his opinion, "the
scholar-critic-professor of literature" is "an ignorant,
self-deceived parasite" who thinks "bourgeois culture
. . . superior to proletarian culture" because in him "bourgeois criteria are completely internalized" by graduate
school indoctrination. This parasite regards as "beyond the
pale" such works as "folk-songs, mysteries, westerns,
science fiction. . . . the most influential and the most
widely controversial American poet—Bob Dylan," to say
nothing of the writings of Mao, "who tells [the people]
that they are the real heroes of history, and that it's right to
rebel because the earth belongs to the people." Instead, he
makes them read T. S. Eliot, "who tells them that they are
trash stuffed with straw, or Jonathan Swift, who tells them
that they are shit-smeared monkeys." (Could so perfect an
echo of old-time Stalinism be a "put-on"? No matter. We
hear the like uttered seriously again all around us.)

Finally, there is the non-literary version of all this,
the recent announcements that "objectivity" in history or
sociology or even science is an illusion accepted only by the
naive or the unscrupulous. Here is Professor Martin
Nicolaus, of the Sociology Liberation Group, "telling it like
it is" at a Plenary Session of the American Sociological
Association in Boston, on August 26, 1968. (His talk is
reprinted in *The American Sociologist* of May, 1969.)

> This assembly . . . is a conclave of high and low
> priests, scribes, intellectual valets, and their inno-
> cent victims, engaged in the mutual affirmation of

> a falsehood, in common consecration of a myth.
> Sociology is not now and never has been any kind
> of objective seeking out of social truth or reality.
> Historically, the profession is an outgrowth of
> nineteenth-century European traditionalism and
> conservatism, wedded to twentieth-century cor-
> poration liberalism. . . . Sociologists stand guard
> over the garrison and report to its masters on the
> movements of the occupied populace.

And again I can show how such stuff filters down to
daily university life by quoting from a memo. This one was
written by several younger university teachers to "expose"
a chairman who had voted against the reappointment of a
new teacher he claimed was incompetent. Their charge is
that he voted as he did because the teacher in question was
an admitted Communist, that it was a "political firing."
Not that the chairman knew what he was doing. Rather,
like a novelist being seen through by a certain kind of
Marxist critic, he was compelled by determining factors of
which he was unaware, though his young critics could see
them plain.

> Professor ––– contends that his decision to
> fire ––– was taken solely for professional reasons.
> In one sense, this is clearly true. We doubt that he
> deliberately set out to purge the ––– Department
> of Communists. Nevertheless, we believe that the
> decision was a political act, a characteristic expres-
> sion of the liberal point of view prevalent in
> American universities and in the society as a
> whole. Given this orientation, was able to arrive at
> what he felt was an academic evaluation without
> understanding its fundamentally political nature.

Interestingly enough, while this inability to be objective is injustice in the liberal, it is virtue in the Marxist. For,
to the charge that the teacher had imposed an a priori
ideological line on the material studied in class, the memo
replies, "how can a Marxist scholar, who proceeds systematically from a set of basic assumptions about society,
politics, and history, avoid the charge of 'imposing a priori
a particular ideological line' on the material in question?
How can a scholar who adopts a throughly critical view of
American society escape the allegation that his perpective is

'closed,' in other words, that he is hopelessly biased?"

Now, if the mind were so reliably dominated by class or race or ideology, it would be hard to understand why liberals, Communists, white men, black men differ among themselves. (Even militant black men—James Baldwin, in spite of the sacrifice of his talent he has made to the cause of black rebellion, is insultingly rejected by Eldridge Cleaver.) The fact is, of course, the automatic recoil of some of us from such views results from our sense that they are distorting the fundamental realities on which the intellectual life is based. It's true, these people tend to make brief parenthetical bows in their direction—for example, that Afro-American Society memo, amid its assertions of white incapacity to understand black writing, actually declares, "We do not intend to argue against the substantial universality of all good literature." But, as we see, "taking for granted" such realities often means, in practice, not only misunderstanding but even contradicting them. Or else it turns out that they are not pertinent *in the present crisis.* Needless to say, the postponing of intel-lectual—and moral—scrupulousness to a time more con-venient is an old story. The time is rarely convenient for those who are avid for chic or simple solutions to complex problems.

The chief error of people like those I've quoted is that they deny to the human mind the autonomy which, in spite of "conditioning," it never ceases to possess. While in the grip of their theories, they don't actually listen to what novelists (or sociologists or teachers) have to say. Instead they eavesdrop on them for a few easily identifiable clues to "real" motives and meanings which are presumed to be consciously or unconsciously concealed. And what is worse, they eavesdrop not in search of the truth, but only to confirm certain theories of what a work *must* be about—be-cause of its author's conditioning—which they had arrived at before looking at it.

Their authorization for assuming such breathtaking superiority to the whole world of gifted people comes first from a simplified idea of science in general (all men are "determined," all acts and thoughts have prior "causes"); and then, in particular, from the guides presumed to be given to those causes by Marx (economic or class interest is the determinant) or Freud (sexual trauma is the determinant) or lately Fanon (men's relation to colonial power is the determinant—a nationalist adaptation of Marx). Armed with those guides, any second-rate would-be critic can dispense with the job of trying to understand the terms and structures of meaning which the writer himself has worked out to express his ideas or to body forth his vision. Brushing these aside, he notes the clues, he applies his ready-made system of interpretation, and he *knows*.

The error here is not in assuming the mind is "determined," but in assuming we can know what determines it and where it must come out. The truth is, of course, the human mind, though no more unconditioned than anything else in the universe, is free at least from the possibility of ever being understood as science understands the motions of physical bodies, understood so as to be predictable. This for two reasons that ought to be obvious, yet somehow keep being forgotten. First, because of the multiplicity, variety, and subtlety of its determining stimuli. Do you think you know what must shape the feelings and ideas of all American Negroes, and that you are entitled to speak of "the" black man and how he must differ from "the" white? Here is a comment on such presumption from Albert Murray, a black critic whose new book *The Omni-Americans* ranks with Ellison's *Shadow and Act* in its liberating common sense on the subject of race and culture. He is responding to Gordon Parks' account of his own life as conditioned by his black background.

Yes. *Of course,* his actions are conditioned by the experience of his U.S. Negro background. What the hell else he going to operate out of? ... [But] the background experience of U.S. Negroes is a rich source of many things ... [not only] frustration and crime, degradation, emascu-

lation, and self-hatred . . . [which may result
from] all human circumstances . . . Nobody who is
really and truly interested in the perpetually
fascinating mystery of human motive and conduct
is ever likely to ignore the fact that many of the
non-Negroes who infest Greenwich Village, the
Bowery, and the narcotic dens of the Upper West
Side often came from a background of freedom
and even wealth and power. . . In spite of all the
substandard test scores, anybody who assumes
that the average white U.S. schoolboy is really
closer to the classics. . . than the average U.S.
Negro schoolboy is either talking about the relative percentage of literary snobs or is simply
kidding himself. A white schoolboy may be
persuaded to bone up and pass a formal exam on,
say, metaphysical poetry, but that doesn't actually
mean he gives a damn about it. A Negro boy, on
the other hand, might well have a genuine feeling
for the blues, which certainly represent an indig-
enous "substitute" for certified high culture
poetry.

One can grant—and Murray doesn't fail to insist—that
American Negroes suffer "brutal restrictions." Still, after
such a glimpse of the real world, of the mysterious, various,
unfashionable ways conditioning really works, where would
be the usefulness in solemnly declaring that "no person has
the ability to stand outside his own conditioning"?

The second reason we must regard the human mind as
free—free at least of any danger that its operations can be
predicted—is that it responds to stimuli in ways that are not
to be explained by the nature of the stimuli alone, in ways
that grow out of its own nature. This idea, I gather, is at the
bottom of the view of mental growth of Jerome Bruner,
who speaks of the ability we have "to exercise initiative,
turn round on our information, reorder it, and generate
hypotheses," an ability that comes from the "productive,
generative structures" in our minds. At any rate, it seems
clear enough that we have evolved out of the mind's own
ways of dealing with the world a number of techniques of
guiding and correcting its operations which are, if not

wholly, at least to a significant degree independent of social background. We see them in the sciences; we see them in the various artistic media and genres. This is why one who devotes himself to an intellectual discipline finds that the discipline itself leads him to perspectives, discriminations, combinations he could not have foreseen. This is why a novelist often discovers his true subject and theme—and, it may be, even with surprise or dismay—in the process of struggling to turn the raw material of his life into a valid work of art. And here I could of course quote Henry James, for whom "art makes life," but since it may be feared that his views reflect the rotten values of a dying bourgeoisie, I turn instead to that other victim of racist bourgeois culture I've mentioned, Ralph Ellison. He is speaking in *Shadow and Act* of what happened when he began to learn something of "the craft and intention of modern poetry and fiction."

> The more I learned of literature in this conscious way, the more the details of my background became transformed. I heard undertones in re-membered conversations which had escaped me before, local customs took on a more universal meaning, values which I hadn't understood were revealed; some of the people whom I had known were diminished while others were elevated in stature. More important, I began to see my own possibilities with more objective, and in a way, more hopeful eyes.

He tells us further that in acquiring technique a novelist is

> learning to conceive of human values in ways which have been established by the great writers who have developed and extended the art. . . . It is technique which transforms the individual before he is able to transform it. And in that personal transformation he discovers something else; he discovers that he has taken on certain obligations, that he must not embarrass his chosen form, and that in order to avoid this, he must develop taste. He learns—and this is most discouraging—that he is involved with values which turn in their own way, and not in the way of politics, upon the central issues affecting his nation and his time.

There is a third fact ignored by those others which I'll
come to in a moment. But these first two alone are surely
of decisive importance. Isn't it because we are thus
"conditioned" by a virtual infinity of factors, inner and
outer, and because our minds add to the this complexity by
reacting in their own way upon these factors, that we can
learn from each other? Isn't this the reason our men of
talent do come up with fresh ideas, just as our good
teachers (and students) do teach us things, instead of
merely giving out what was put in a class or race or the
Zeitgeist? Actually, when not defending some theory, we
all know this. We all know that each person is a new world
of unique experience, or of common experience in unique
degrees and combinations, and that it is out of these new
worlds that the fountain of human creations issues which
forever enriches or confuses our lives.

But to recognize the uniqueness of each man is to be
brought up against a question. How can unique beings
communicate with each other, and, what is stranger still,
communicate across the additional barriers of race, class,
nation, and even centuries? Or are the Gilmans and Kampfs
right who, for their own reasons, say they have ceased to do
so? Well, we have to begin, of course, with the undoubted
fact that they do. The ancient Greek Sophocles, the
eleventh-century Japanese Lady Murasaki, the Renaissance
Englishman Shakespeare, the nineteenth-century Russian
Dostoevsky—as well as philosophers and sages similarly
remote from mid-twentieth-century Americans—do make
sense to us, even to some of us under thirty. Reading them
we do understand better our own natures and possibilities.
The reason for this—and here is that third fact—was
suggested long ago by Montaigne: *Chaque homme port la
forme entiere de l'humaine condition.* I take this to
imply that all, or at least myriads, of human possibilities
exist within each of us, waiting to be lifted into consciousness by the precisely appropriate circumstances or suggestions. A seeming paradox follows, which is the basis of art as
it is of most human relationships. The only way to get at

interests in common with members of his own group which
he is less likely to have in common with outsiders. It is also
true that one's class, say, or generation will set limits to
what he will experience, think and produce. But the
interests and limitations one shares with others in a group,
however useful to sociology, which deals mainly in general-
ized images of man, cannot reveal what he is in his own
particular being. For, as already implied, each individual is
black, white, Jew, WASP, or of the Romantic Period in his
own way, never the simple duplicate of his fellow group
members. And because it is only in the unique particulars
of a man's nature which elude all such wholesale cate-

gories that we come close to the man himself, it is only in them—that paradox again—that we touch the common human potentiality which those particulars alone body forth. On the last page of *Mimesis*, his magnificent reading of the central works of the Western tradition of realism, Eric Auerbach explains this paradox in his own way as he tells how mimetic art, precisely because it brings us so close to the actual lives of individuals, has led us more and more to recognize the oneness of man. The purpose of such art becoming, he says,

> to put the emphasis on the random occurrence, to exploit it not in the service of a planned continuity of action but in itself. And in the process something new and elemental appeared: nothing less than the wealth of reality and depth of life in every moment to which we surrender ourselves without prejudice. To be sure, what happens in that moment—be it outer or inner processes— concerns in a very personal way the individuals who live in it, but it also (and for that very reason) concerns the elementary things which men in general have in common. It is precisely the random moment which is comparatively independent of the controversial and unstable orders over which men fight and despair; it passes unaffected by them, as daily life. The more it is exploited the more the elementary things which our lives have in common come to light.

But I said there was some truth in those misleading and dangerous notions. First—and this may sound for a moment like a contradiction—it does after all make sense to talk of black (or Jewish or Irish) literature as having a character of its own. The author of these lines has himself been known to deny that a non-Jew can ever fully share his pleasure in Sholom Aleichem. Similarly, one must expect that black men, or Irishmen, reading together a work by one of themselves, are likely to exchange pleased glances at times when we others are merely getting the main idea. But this must be understood correctly. If a writer's fidelity to the particulars of his experience will turn up many details and expressions only his kin will enjoyably *remember*, surely any fiction which offers nothing but the pleasure of such literal accuracy, which does not at the same time put its particulars into some illuminating relationship with each other and thus enable us to recognize an underlying truth, is second-rate. (I don't speak of poetry, in which the language itself, and even the reader's memory of its unique history, are central to the experience, and which is simply closed to those who are not intimate with the language.) If Sholom Aleichem is a great writer, it is because his ability to convey the particulars of Jewish experience and modes of response is matched by his power to show them as *ways to be human.* There is, as a matter of fact, a deeper way to understand the ethnic character of a literature. The experience and traditions common to a group may well account for the predominance among them of certain ways of being human rather than others, just as, in the individual writer, illness or wealth or some other personal pressure may account for the kinds of reality he is led to feel most sharply and therefore to make most vivid to us. But the "strangeness" of a foreign culture, like that of a single original writer, is not a barrier. On the contrary, it introduces us, if we have the capacity for deepening self-awareness, to the unexplored possibilities of our own nature. For this reason, first-rate writing by black Americans—for instance, *The Autobiography of Malcolm X*—should be not only intelligible to whites, but a required part of their education. To quote Ellison again, "The small share of reality which each of our diverse groups is able to snatch from the whirling chaos of history belongs not to the group alone, but to all of us. It is a property and a witness which can be ignored only to the danger of the entire nation."

But there is another apparent contradiction to face up to, even more troublesome. It has to be granted that such emphasis on the universal may diminish our power to see and value the particular forms in which it is always expressed, and thus bleach life of its color, its charm. One must go even further. Spinoza says somewhere that God

does not generalize—He sees only fact. That is, the
particular concrete fact is never wholly expressed except by
itself; all generalizations are approximate. And this means
that, after all, it would be wrong—it would be a kind of
intellectual hubris—to forget that every human being
remains in certain ways alone and that no perfect communication is ever possible. Well, yes. But though that is
true, it is also true that language and culture exist, and that
we have built great cities together, and great literatures. We
have had pleasure and solace from friends. The irreducible
residue of the inexpressible in men and experience should
not lead us to undervalue such communion as is possible. It
is with this communion-that-is-possible that all the world's
work is done. In any case, it is not by the stereotypes of
race or politics that we are led to confront the actual
difference and mystery of a man. By those stereotypes the
real man is obliterated.

Then we must grant that even for that foolish turning
away in colleges from Pope or Proust, the "Western
masterpieces" generally, there is a certain justification. It is
regrettably true that literary works have been made to *seem*
irrelevant because they have been taught in ways that
reduce them to less than they are and that inhibit, rather
than promote, a genuine experience of them. In this "age of
criticism" from which we are now perhaps emerging, too
many English teachers, applying mechanically the lore
gathered in graduate school, or the hints of gifted critics,
have yielded to the temptation to play the expert and to
make little experts of their students. The works of
literature ostensibly being studied have been replaced by
theories, theories oriented toward technique, myth,
symbol, "scientific" categories, and the like. Aside from the
fact that this turns literature into a bore, there are two
unfortunate results of such "pretense of expertise." One is
that it often prevents the more accurate knowledge it
claims to ensure. For the only reliable method of dealing

with literature, as Eliot has said, is to be very intelligent, which I take to mean not to avoid theory—we can't do that—but to hold theories lightly in our hand, like tools that may at any moment, amid the fluid complexities of literature and of our relationship to it, cease to be appropriate; in other words, to stay open to the as yet *unaccredited* responses and insights of fresh experience. But the second result of the pretense of expertise is worse. It is that it usually rules out of order our own and our students' personal relation with the non-literary, the human core of literary works. It thus inhibits that more conscious concern with life which is surely a chief reward of the study of literature.

But even granting that the classroom should be, as too often it has not been, a place where we try to engage in a genuinely living relationship with literature, why does it follow that we have to remove from it all works that come to us from distant times, places, social classes—except as instructive examples of the *other*—and replace them by works that come from or apply directly to our own? Why is it necessary to enliven the class with titillating pseudo-therapy or to borrow excitement for the dull old text from the issues of the hour? Far from making the study of literature more relevant, such tricks simply distract attention from that true relevance—to our humanity—which is precisely what enables certain books to live past their own time, and which they retain long after all local or fashionable reasons for interest in them have disappeared. (Speaking thus to "the more elementary things which men in general have in common," they will apply often enough, of course, to the issues of the hour, though they may not be useful to narrow partisans.) Strange that one should need to say this to English teachers, but our job is surely to help students see and feel that true relevance, that permanent power of first-rate literature to move and liberate us, which makes our "great books" the richest legacy of human history.

As for the denial of the possibility of objectivity, this seems to me, as I have suggested, only another version of

the idea that men can't step outside their conditioning. It is
a truth, but, in its current, mainly political application a
useless and misleading truth. For after all, we don't really
require any chemical purity from conditioning—or subjectivity—in order to make a distinction between the true and
the false the honest man and the cheat. It is enough to
grant first, that some people deliberately lie to gain private
ends, while others want no private advantage that is not
based on as much truth as possible; and second, that for
those who seek the truth there are ways, in art and the
other humanities, as well as in science, to increase significantly the reality content of their thought. This being the
case, to emphasize our irremediable subjectivity often
sounds suspiciously like a useful alibi for liars.

The fact is, for too many of the intellectuals of the
New Left the denial of the possibility of objectivity, of a
significant, if partial, freedom from the "conditioning" of
race or class or generation, is not a reasoned position but a
strategy for silencing those who are in danger of thinking
for themselves. The argument goes like this: There is a
battle in progress for bread and justice. All you writers and
teachers, and the works you place before us, must
inevitably serve either the oppressors or their victims.
Therefore, give up the pretense or illusion that you have
anything of your own to say, or that you can lead to insight
which men of differing political persuasions can respect.
Instead, join us, and in your work openly express those
correct ideas which we already possess.

Now obviously, the world we live in is not what it
should be, and intelligent social protest is very much in
order. There is a battle going on for bread and justice,
which are everywhere inequitably distributed. The situation
of black Americans is still a disgrace to the nation, in spite
of progress. Our brutal intervention in the Vietnamese civil
war is a shame and a horror. And though such demands on
our conscience may be used as pretexts by the foolish or
the unscrupulous, yet the demands have a real basis. For
this reason, certain questions are bound to haunt all of us

engaged in intellectual work. If we must be left free in
order to make the most of the mind's wealth of unpredictable possibilities, and if, in this freedom, the principles and
methods of our work must sometimes be permitted to lead
us away from the immediate interests of our fellows, may
not this truth too be used as a pretext? May it not be used
as a cover for the wish to stay safe while others risk their
necks? More precisely, since our work requires peace and
quiet and regular meals, may not a refusal to join some
battle for social justice be motivated by a fear of reprisals
from the powers, not always just, which supply them? To
such questions one must uncomfortably assent. That can
happen. But again we must be careful in seeing what
follows. It surely does not follow that intellectual principles
and methods—the "Mediterranean" values of reason, and so
on—and those who try to live by them have become agents
of oppression or obsolete. If some men of mind are venal
and cowardly, others are not. Since the time of Socrates,
reason and art have also opposed the "establishment" and
found for its victims. Indeed, a good case is often made
for the view that No! in thunder, or in whispers, is what
reason and art usually say to things as they are, and say it
on behalf of that better way they ought to be which is the
ultimate goal of the social engineers.

The essential difference between those who would
remain faithful to the principles and methods of art and
thought—say, a university faculty of the kind that used to
be admired—and those who join the social or political battle
is not that one group is escaping to an ivory tower and
serving only themselves (or the "establishment") and the
other confronting reality and serving their fellow men. It is
that the first wish to remain open to new ideas and to
protect the conditions out of which they come, while the
"militants" tend to think they have as much truth as they
need. It is also that the former, as a class, serve men in the
whole range of their needs, serve that Ideal City (never to

be reached, though the struggle toward it can enrich our lives) which will be the home of man's fullest development; and the latter serve men in the short run and the pressing needs of the moment. Undoubtedly, both kinds of service have their place, and occasions do arrive when those who are capable of action had better act. But we must all decide for ourselves how much of our time and energy we owe to each. What we must not do, and what the social engineer ought not to demand that we do, is import into the study or classroom attitudes appropriate to the political arena, which too often means simplify or distort the complex truth to attain some "practical" goal. We must try not to sacrifice for immediate ends any power we have to serve the deeper needs of men that go on forever. Those who demand such a sacrifice—imposing the unreal alternatives "with us or against us," prating of "art for the people," and claiming to scorn the "elitism" of intellectual, artistic, and sometimes even moral standards—are not really being practical and honest as against the escapist and hypocritical others. Instead, they are rejecting—with the practicality of Stalinists or Nazis—the habits of mind by which free men will be able to judge and resist them. And sometimes, too, they are taking the revenge of the mediocre on the gifted, and using social crisis as an alibi for rejecting standards they are incapable of meeting.

I conclude by summing up. It is not true that the intellectual life is a battle of brute self-interest, and that men cannot speak to each other over the barriers imposed by their origins. This recurrent idea is contradicted by the nature of the human mind and the fact of the human community. For the mind is not the puppet of a few obvious conditions, but is shaped by unknowable myriads and in some degree selects or makes its own. And our fellowship with men of other races, nations and times is brought home to us by our continual recognition of ourselves in their works. We know what men may and should become in large part because we see what they have been.

Granted that insistence on the human community can be used to stifle legitimate protest ("Though you have nothing, and I everything, don't be rude, we're brothers underneath"). But the denial of it can be used to impose totalitarian despotism ("Men are divided by class or race, to disagree with us is to be our enemy, lock him up!"). In the same way, an exclusive emphasis on the universal will lead us away from reality, and equally an exclusive emphasis on the particular. And though it is difficult to avoid both kinds of error, that happens to be the necessary job of those of us who would do justice to the works of human intellect. Or would serve our fellows in all the variety of their needs, and serve them without making them pay—as certain kinds of "idealists" always do—by giving up their freedom or part of their mind.

The Real Generation Gap

By Franklin Chu

I thought that the only generation gap was between me and my father until I talked to a freshman. Far from feeling like a senior dispensing wisdom to a freshman, I realized that he knew as much as I did. Freshmen now enter Harvard blase about the things that jolted me and my classmates out of adolescence; as a result they breeze through the traditional four-year Harvard experience in a year or less. For the remainder of college they face a wildly different experience. Their new standards, what they expect from themselves, from Harvard, and from their futures, will define this experience and inevitably change Harvard itself.

For the present this revolution in standards creates a generation gap between upperclassmen and underclassmen who find it difficult to relate to each other because they think so differently. Attitudes toward drugs and politics most clearly indicate this rift. One freshman user from California talked to me as if I were three decades rather than three years older than he:

"Do you take drugs?" I ventured.

(Laugh) "Who doesn't?"

"Well, what do you take?"

"That's the wrong question, Frank. You have to ask when I took what. There's been a whole dope cycle.

Acid was the beautiful drug of the past, but now a lot of people are scared because a bad trip can really mess you up. Mescaline is a popular replacement. Speed and smack are coming in too."

"Smack?"

"Slang for heroin."

"Oh."

"Then there's the *bella donna*, the ultimate trip. You have to have someone with you to give you the antidote or you don't come down . . . until you're dead. I've never done that, but I do a lot of social smoking."

Remembering the pot parties of my freshman and sophomore years, I responded, "Right, you mean with girls, music, and strobes?"

"No, that's teeny-bopper tripping. I mean sharing joints with good friends minus the lights and music. You also have to distinguish social smoking from psycho-ward tripping in the winter when it's shit outside and you stay in the dorm with nothing to stare at but the walls."

Politics emphasizes the generation gap in a more direct way. My question to a Marxist freshman from New York City about upperclassmen provoked a pole-mic against older radicals, who he complained were "too involved with themselves and held haphazard relation-ships with other students." Though optimistic about the radical movement as a whole, he deplored SDS for "degenerating into a system of heavyweights—upperclassmen clustering tight little groups around them." He argued that freshmen could avoid the mis-takes of upperclassmen by putting all their knowledge into practice.

Not all freshmen take such a dim view, if indeed they have a view, of older radicals, but many of them share a disillusionment with Harvard. Their cynicism, nurtured by early high school political activity and con-firmed by the ill-fated strike of April 1969, pierced the Harvard aura their first semester. They quickly grasped that a few departments are terrible, the tutorial system inadequate, a program in creative arts non-existent, and the administration not very responsive to suggested changes. One freshman summed up the attitude of his classmates between sips of coffee in the Freshman Union, "We expected Harvard to be mediocre and it is."

Mediocrity was what my classmates and I thought we had left behind when we came to Harvard in the fall of 1966, the year Barry Sadler's *The Ballad of the Green Berets* was number one on the hit parade. One drama activist, who had the longest hair in Cambridge before it was sheared for his fiancee's parents, sheepishly admitted, "I thought Harvard was going to be a place of immense opportunity, freedom—a Mecca. [Embarrassed silence.] I even conceived of myself as the Renaissance man, well-rounded and learned in various areas." His conceptions were shared by a good many of our classmates. Sure that Harvard offered wonderful opportunities, we felt it our duty to take advantage of them and vowed to accomplish something. Not surprisingly, our Harvard experience turned into a four-year ego-trip.

At first freshman year was ego shattering. Our high school identities ceased to hold meaning: 800 board scores, newspaper editorships, student council presidencies and all-state football honors made us part of the crowd rather than distinguished from it. Only the true cosmopolitans and fiercely motivated academics safely retained their identities. One good friend of mine had gone to prep school in Switzerland and worked for a year in Africa as a journalist; he was self-confident enough to sail serenely through freshman year. Another decided that he loved Anglo-Saxon poetry and dismissed what his peers were doing.

The rest of us struggled to establish our identities. With accomplishment as our goal we continually experimented to find our "thing." Some tried out for the

Harvard Lampoon, cracked bad jokes to the members, and woke up at 7 A.M. to perform calisthenics. Others competed for the *Crimson*, staying up all night as trial night editors while their own pieces were getting torn apart. Another started shooting a film though he had never before worked a camera. Still another set out on an odyssey up and down the East Coast with his rock band, almost ending up in a group marriage with a girl from Florida, a girl from New York, and a guy from Boston. A few, like myself, decided to give our egos a rest and took a year off. Those who stayed soon burrowed into little niches, assuming their proper role and contributing to the famous Harvard diversity.

My class would have continued in the traditional Harvard experience had not the swelling protest against ROTC on campus and the demands of the black students for Afro-American courses burst into the violent strike in April 1969. Its impact was far greater on us than on underclassmen, for we were set in what we were doing and secure about what we thought of Harvard. Suddenly we became embroiled in something where nobody knew what was coming off. For the first time we enjoyed becoming part of a mass, joining the fifteen thousand students who met in Harvard Stadium and the thousands more crowded into Memorial Church. Those never politically involved found themselves passing out leaflets for SDS. Enthusiasm, even jubilation, permeated that week in April. But Harvard the institution completely dismayed us. Fair Harvard was not only unfair, but irresponsible and vindictive. The bludgeoning of students in University Hall tumbled my classmates out of their niches into common disillusionment and depression.

When I came back in the fall of 1969 from my year in Paris, I was struck by the large number of my classmates who had withdrawn into themselves. Not knowing anymore what they wanted to do, they shunned all that they didn't want to do. Avoiding hassle, simplifying life was everybody's thing. A friend wanted to move off campus, ostensibly to write his senior thesis in privacy, but spent most of his time brooding or machinating to avoid the draft. An ex-roommate moved out of Cambridge into the neighboring suburb of Somerville and spent his days writing plays and poetry. He rarely went to the campus. To my question about what he thought of freshmen, he replied ruefully, "I know as much about freshmen as a forty-year-old man."

Suspecting that I knew as little about freshmen as he did I spent the following week rapping with them. I didn't have to go to Mississippi to find another country; I stumbled into the dorms in Harvard Yard where all the freshmen live. The inhabitants of the Yard haven't changed from previous years (the Admissions Committee guarantees an almost identical annual mix), but the ways they judge their classmates and themselves, what they think and want from Harvard, and how they foresee their futures have radically changed. A silent revolution—a revolution in student standards—has transpired.

One of the most noticeable new standards is how freshmen judge each other. My classmates acknowledged the admirable fellow (we're too arrogant to have campus heroes) with a "God, he's bright!" In contrast, freshmen admire a classmate because "God, he's a good guy!" The good guy is someone who radiates good "vibes" (vibrations) to others and is not psychotic about doing his own thing. His first priority is his community of friends, and he measures himself more by what he contributes to the group than by his own accomplishments. One of these good guys explained to me, "The emphasis has switched from producing a work of art to making yourself a work of art."

I don't normally think of Harvard Yard as a gallery of art, but certainly informal groups of people grooving together—a rare occurrence my year there—have sprung up all around. Even the feeling of being in a group is different. When we were together we had to assert our own individuality or, paradoxically, not make it as part of the group. Freshmen are much less hung-up about communication. Bullshitting one night with a bunch of freshmen in Grey's Hall, I finally got an idea what it's like to be a member of the gang.

The shift in standards also alters what freshmen want from Harvard. Many arrived knowing what they didn't want to do, something we didn't realize until after our frenzy to do just about everything. Yet the number of freshmen who are aware of their values and know what they want to do is staggering. It's even frightening, for the most earnest and arrogant among them would disregard all conflicting opinions had they the chance to transform Harvard according to their perspectives. One freshmen from a radical high school wants to politicize Harvard completely. "There's no such thing as a neutral academic institution. Harvard serves clearly defined interests. I want to end Harvard's corporate interests and make it a counter-institution disseminating revolutionary thought—to take Harvard apart piece by piece and put it together again." Another freshman, certain that he will be a photographer, said of Harvard: "I take out what's relevant to me—like using physical facilities and reading social thinkers who interest me. I didn't come to Harvard to grow as a person . . . No one should come to Harvard who doesn't know what he wants to do." Harvard used to give its students a perspective on life, if nothing else. Now freshmen enter Harvard already equipped with a world view and think not what Harvard can do *for* them but what they can do *to* Harvard.

Growing numbers of students dismiss Harvard the academic institution as irrelevant. Few freshmen wish to dedicate their lives to academic work; some don't even want to attempt it. One freshman predicted that the number of students concentrating in natural science this fall will be small because many did not bother to take introductory math and science courses in the first place.

More than mulling over courses to take, they consider taking a year off or even dropping out completely. None of the seven or eight freshmen in Grey's Hall whom I asked expected to graduate with his class. One admitted, "I didn't expect to last more than two months." His reason for not having left was the hassle of moving his junk back to California. But he was quick to add, "I certainly won't be back next year."

Accent on community life, a cynicism about what Harvard has to offer, and a future not determined by academic work and the university make up the revolution in standards, but what are its causes? One, already mentioned, is the greater sophistication of freshmen. Eighteen is so much older now than it was before; freshmen don't need college to help them grow up. Drugs more than deans influence their lives and their college experience. Unlike writing or studying, taking drugs is a group activity. During the first semester, freshmen get to know each other by sharing a joint. Entire dorm entry ways of thirty guys turn on together. One freshman in Matthews Hall extolled the community spirit engendered when the entry crowded into his room every night to smoke. In addition to bringing groups of students together, drugs affect the individual's mind and his outlook toward others. All freshmen I talked to claimed that tripping made them aware how much they needed other people and increased their sensitivity to them. One went so far as to say that he can tell who has and who hasn't tripped by the way they respond to people. The culture which surrounds the use of drugs provides a unifying bond for freshmen that my class never had.

The main cause of the revolution in standards is probably the existence of an Alternate Culture. The underground of drop-outs and drop-ins traveling in small groups or living in large communes has risen to the very visible foreground. No longer is life simply a choice between college and a job. Join the Alternate Culture

and you can float up, up and away with others like you. One Harvard drop-out married a Brazilian girl on one of his foreign haunts and works in a fish factory in New England when he needs bread. Another left for Micronesia, adopted a little Micronesian boy, and is now back in the States being a stepfather. There is little difficulty finding a place to live, for communes are springing up all over the country and may someday be as ubiquitous as Burger King. Dropping out isn't very frightening anymore; it might be best for those with no desire to pursue the academic life or join the Establishment.

Student standards have changed in part because their parents' standards have changed. Generation gap books and articles too often portray parents as dogmatic, unchanging, untrustworthy dolts. Harvard parents aren't stupid (most of them went to Harvard and Radcliffe, too) and they have evolved along with their children, putting less pressure on them to succeed or adjust to a society which embodies few of their values. One freshman whose older brother went to Yale remarked about his parents, "After my brother they know better than to bug me. They're even beginning to understand me." Parents, it seems, are beginning to apply Dr. Spock's permissiveness to their college-age sons.

Increasing parental permissiveness along with early maturity, the prevalence of drugs, and the existence of an Alternate Culture, because of their influence on so many students, have curiously brought an end to diversity in the freshman class. Many of the freshman proctors I met referred to the "greater homogeneity of this year's freshman class." One proctor explained to me, "Of course, not all freshmen are drug freaks or radicals. But they do have a common culture binding them. They're much more alike than when I went to Harvard a few years ago." As a common culture engulfs students, niches become harder to find. No longer can one be a Poonie, a Crimed, a Loebie, a jock, a science wonk, or a clubbie. Such types have ceased to exist except in the imagination of a few students mired in the mythical Harvard past. One of these students happens to be a friend—he admits he is a rarity. Shortly after last April's strike, he decided he had had enough contact with the masses, rushed to join a club, religiously learned the elements of good taste, and is now club president. Confiding to me that "I sincerely want to believe in certain Harvard myths," he fondly recalled the days when one never left the clubhouse and mourned, "There're no beautiful people left."

With the exodus of the beautiful people and a generation gap among present upperclassmen and underclassmen, whither Harvard? One possibility is that the Harvard experience may be shortened to one week: freshmen will arrive, become disoriented, and leave. Another possibility, if admissions policies don't change, is that Harvard will become exceedingly straight. Many of the brightest and hippest kids aren't going through the motions that get you into Harvard—like grubbing for A's and joining absurd extracurricular activities. If this happens, and Establishment-oriented kids enter Harvard, no doubt this year's freshmen will encounter a generation gap with those future freshmen. That will serve them right for making me feel like an old man.

The Unity Game –
Reflections of a
Faculty Moderate

By Benjamin DeMott

ONE HUNDRED ON COLUMBIA FACULTY URGE
STRONG ACTION TO HALT [CLASS] DISRUPTERS

—headline from *The New York Times*
March 11, 1969

—End-of-summer picnic in a college town near
Amherst. N., last seen in June, comes by with
coffee and asks about the Columbia faculty unity
statement—the one signed and circulated by
Trilling, Hofstadter, Barzun and ninety-seven
others last spring. Did the xerox he mailed ever
arrive? What did I think? Spiky, distant, I back
off, hide behind The Summer. I am depressed
just by the reminder of that time—events
at "our" college. "We" cooled a student strike
into a "moratorium," then wrote a letter to Nixon
explaining that our troubles were his fault, then
lifted off on a great blown geyser of media ap-
proval and gamesmanly self-regard. —Too much
going on, I say, summer committees, tons of
mimeo stuff, I'd need to go back and reread the
thing, awful memory . . . Did they have in mind
circulating it, getting the Valley colleges to sign?
(There are now five of us along the Connecticut
River in western Massachusetts.) A steering

committee? Thanks for the nudge, etc., send me
the deadline, etc., sorry, etc., thanks again, etc.

This slipperiness smells—but what can you
do? I remember the document perfectly—an expression of faculty solidarity in the face of student
challenges—"attempts to disrupt or prevent the
holding of classes." Doubtless the sponsors and
signers shook hands all around in August, when
the national student groups announced plans for
fall hell weeks—the Chicago anti-war demon-
stration, the October shutdown by the Student
Mobilization Committee, the student strike and
March on Washington. Members of the academic
community, the statement said, must "accept
their responsibility to protect each other's rights
and demonstrate the will to act. . . . We call
upon all members of this and other universities
to defend by example and by action the fundamental principles of a free university. It is our
intention not to surrender the safeguards of
freedom that men have erected . . . over several
centuries." The document actually came to me
twice—first the xerox from N., and then the
Columbia administration sent it out to alumni
and friends, together with a letter from President
Cordier, saluting this "eloquent indication of
faculty unity" and declaring that "a new spirit
has been created on the campus in which the
sharp and bitter divisions of last spring have disappeared."

It came in twice and in theory should have
been welcome *chez moi*. A "moderate" statement, as they say—firm, not hysterical. A vote
for the faculty interest that transcends individual
campuses. A level of writing far above that of
most faculty statement prose. (". . . The academic community is [not] supine or befuddled
in the face of these challenges." Dean Barzun?

"No genuine education can take place if teachers and students are cast in an adversary role." Professor Trilling?) No attempt to excuse complacency: The statement conceded the need for additional reforms in "university governance," an accompanying letter called for "more informed discussion and considered action . . . to remedy social ills and racial injustice, and to deal with the causes of war," and the text included an allusion to the possibility of faculty-student action in the area of curricular change.

A nd while part of my scratchiness about the document might be laid to diffidence, reluctance to deliver another boring speech on a tattered subject, it wouldn't be a large part. For I'm not a true believer in diffidence in this context. I wince a lot, sure, beg to be spared—but I know people *ought* to talk up, even at the risk of tiresomeness. Many teachers' opinions about "disruption" are grainy, contradictory. The absence outside, among the general public, of any feeling for the graininess hurts. It also hurts inside. Uncertainty and ambiguity about individual faculty opinion are too often the rule: people can't grasp the next man's position, can't feel their way into its intricacies.

And once the crises arrive there's no time for full explanations. Heat's on, a run to moral stereotypes starts, ignorance feeds back. The White House announces that the wars of academe are between "moral arrogance" and cowardice, and overnight everybody's a figure in allegorical tableaux—flat-out face-offs of vice and virtue. Marcuseans call administrators cruel, sadistic repressors. Anti-Marcuseans yap at disrupters as egomaniacs and destroyers or hypocrites and

traitors. Talks that begin with civil criticism of
"egalitarians" or "elitists" zoom in a minute into
damnation of monsters. If you're at the University of Pittsburgh, you see in the paper that your
famous colleague in the philosophy of science,
Adolph Grunebaum, is outraged about a proposal
nobody proposed—he calls it "monstrous." ("It
is monstrous to require professors of surgery to
base the practice and teaching of their subject
on a majority vote of the fourth-year medical
students.") If you're at Rutgers, you hear a
younger man—Richard Koffler—insisting that
yesterday a faculty majority proved itself to be
selfish, racist, in league with South Africa. (This
was said after a tentative vote—reversed in a day
or two—against admitting "underqualified Negroes.") The notion of being precise about
who's fighting whom—or about what the opponents truly want—is thrown out as a trick, a
strategy of delay.

—No, I believe (repeat) that people should
spell themselves out. The only question is: Can
a man represent himself fairly in quick party
chat? At the picnic I doubted it. A minor qualm
or two could have been shed—as, for example, that I was put off by the closed-in, on-this-rock-we-rest character of the Columbia statement. You are always looking for a sense of
opening or exploration. You know why it's not
there—Columbia has Had It—but still it isn't
there, and (sorry), not seeing it bugs me . . .
That's first and easiest. But as for the rest—

The rest takes more than a minute. The gist
of it is this: The avowed intent of the Columbia
statement was to assert the teacher's right to
determine his subjects and modes of discourse
in accordance with his own best professional
judgment—no interference, no bullying. But an

indirect effect of the document was to endorse
the Class, the pure, undisruptable, sanctified
MWF 11:00 A.M., as a quasi-"fundamental principle" in itself. Implicit in such endorsements is
the suggestion that present faculty differences
about the uses of immediate experience in a
teaching/learning community (not to mention
differences about whether the right to dictate the
terms of the learning situation must forever rest,
non-negotiably, with the faculty) are a negligible
item, no barrier to unity. And that suggestion is
wrong.

True enough, majority power still resides
with the faction that regards classes and courses
and reported experience as the only appropriate
centers of intellectual activity in a university.
But a resistance movement does exist, and the
developing struggle between the two forces needs
to come farther into the open, partly because it
will help to revitalize and redefine the fundamental principles, partly because postponing an
address to issues of life-reference is likely to increase disruption instead of diminishing it.

Is my point over-obvious? If you bundle it
into the too-familiar bag with lectures about
relevance and interdiscipline-ism, of course it is.
Once dumped there, it appears to be one more
manifestation of the new jockery or redskinism,
one more adaptation of the worn theme of education as moral self-improvement, one more
ground for rapping critics of the status quo as
characters devoid of intellectual dignity. As
every schoolboy knows, rapping in that vein lately grows shriller. Across the field stretching from
Jacques Barzun to Karl Shapiro to Edward Shils
you hear about "opportunists" or about grown

men "sucking up to the kids" or about over-per-
missivism and "treachery to the disciplines"—
and about neurotics, new populists, library
burners, pro-illiterates, etc. Often the explicit
charge is that the life-reference man is too
ignorant to know the purposes served by distributing inquiry into manageable fields, by developing bodies of knowledge transmittable in a
classroom context. Repeatedly, teachers of substantial accomplishment find themselves obliged
to swear their allegiance to high intellectual
standards before they can go on to remind listen-
ers that the artificiality of fields is too easily forgotten, and that the crucial need is for significant
turnings-out from the controlled artificial environment of chair rows, blackboards, reported experience—the "discipline"—toward the texture of
immediacy.

Fortunately, some teachers subject to this
pressure aren't intimidated by it. The critic F. R.
Leavis lectured a university audience quite un-
timidly a few months ago on the wisdom of
abolishing English courses that amount merely
to some poems or novels or authors to be studied,
or that fidget the term away with "practical criticism." The English teacher's proper concern,
Leavis noted, is life itself—wrong to split it up
or shave it down, wrong to leave it out (as many
people do) "because 'it's not really real' or 'it's
too important to matter.'" And with that concern in mind, he proposed a complete revision
of the English major, looking toward a collaboration of teachers and students in day-to-day
evaluation of contemporary communication, expression and personal life—a venture that would
develop standards directly from the tension between lived life and literary versions of human
creativity and social possibility, and that would

not take the inviolable Class as its center.

And dozens of other teachers—"solid," well-respected professionals among them—continue to show comparable irreverence. A sociologist at the University of Pennsylvania—Rolf Meyersohn—publishes a critique of ordinary methods courses in his own subject. Why do teachers slight the truth that working sociologists use many other ways of testing and generating hypotheses besides desk-bound, digit-happy, Census Bureau interview and statistics methodology? Why ignore participant-observer techniques, attempts to learn about communities by studying the moment-to-moment effect of the investigator's own presence in the subject culture? How can justice be done to this kind of inquiry inside the classroom? . . . A brilliant philosophy scholar at Queens College—John McDermott—publishes a fascinating study of American philosophical attitudes toward experience as a teacher. His pugnacious advice is that academic man try another look at Emerson, Dewey, James, Pearce —rediscover what was once made, in intellectual terms, of the method of experience, and perceive not merely the American-ness of the method, but its fruitfulness as well. ("Experience is our only teacher," says Pearce. How does learning occur with such a teacher? "It takes place by a series of surprises.") Should not schools institutionalize the dialectic between experience and disciplinary learning, work it into their deep structure?

There are, to be sure, difficulties and weaknesses on the life-reference or class-disrupting side. "We" are too sociable with the turn-on gang —drug cultists, sex experimenters, antinomians, mysticals, flamboyants, winners like the Wellesley lass at the last commencement who told the audience that she and her pals were out for ecstasy. (Go 'way, parents and teachers, you just can't understand.) And clear lines are rarely drawn—as should be done—between the cause of life-reference education, social revolution, social service, and pacifism.

B ut what matters is that many first-rate people in the academy—professionals who can't be dismissed as mollycoddlers, slobs, sentimentalists, political agitators, misplaced hipsters, hunters of lost youth—now understand that the key issue in academic confrontation concerns the proper relationship between the university and the edge of lived experience. Among these professionals a significant minority is bent, as indicated, on an indecorous gesture against the ancient, hallowed, reported-experience ground— as a way of seeking accreditation for immediate experience. And, owing to the nature of the times, the minority is gaining adherents. Events conspire, seemingly. A book like Moynihan's *Maximum Feasible Misunderstanding* shows readers the bad consequences of public policy that follows a "discipline version" of ghetto needs and ignores lived reality. The media that create "occasions" rather than art objects pull the culture ever more powerfully "into the act." Themes of anti-passivity pass into common parlance from existential writers . . . The life-style of unguardedness, downrightness, anti-decorum, involvement becomes a norm . . .

Would it not be better if the relevant pedagogical issues could be talked out on quiet turf, with no distractions? Certainly—but the circumstances of change can't always be nicely controlled. Creating alternatives to traditional course patterns means—as half a dozen new institutions have learned—inventing new modes of collaborative planning between teachers and students, new lines about admissions, evaluation, every aspect of conventional schooling. These aren't overnight jobs. They are, however, substantial and decent jobs, and facing up to them is a prime academic responsibility. It won't be seen as that, though, if the life-reference cause is deprecated as with-it-ism or whimsy, or smeared as a bullyboy threat to academic freedom. Somewhere in the Columbia document—mainly in the

stony, armored tones of teacherly lordliness—I
heard the old anti-experiential rag. And it was
from that that I backed off.

Well then, says a voice: What should we
conclude? Academic freedom is nowhere en-
dangered? Faculties haven't any business insisting on their intellectual-pedagogical preroga-
tives? No, that's not the claim. The claim—laying
it out again—is that faculty proclamations
shouldn't, obliquely or otherwise, bless pedagogical orthodoxy as the holystone of academic
freedom. What we want is something more
spacious and realistic—an endorsement of faculty
rights that speaks to things as they are, and
eschews the Military Bit (E.M. there, officers
here). Let faculty statements begin with an admission that teachers aren't and can't be and
shouldn't be united in pedagogical theory at this
moment. Let them acknowledge that a fresh
sense of university education is in the air, posing
more than a merely chichi challenge to established forms and procedures and assumptions.
Let it be said that there's an effort on the one
hand to elevate the status of immediate experience, to win acceptance for it as a genuine re-
source in higher learning. Give the petition-
signers a chance to say out loud that multi-track
higher education—partly discipline-oriented,
partly experience-oriented—may well be a good
thing; that in schools to come the line between
classroom and non-classroom experience, intellectual and "merely personal" growth, may be
less boldly drawn; that we're not as certain as in
yesteryear that the conditions necessary and sufficient for a classroom to become a place of learning are inviolability and teacher-domination; and

that our former hierarchy of "places of learning" seems just now rather shaky. (Nobody can learn to edit Persius by living in a halfway house for adolescent delinquent boys; nobody can assess the value of the concept of community, as Moynihan pointed out, merely by poring over Robert A. Nisbet and Paul Goodman in a library; nobody can confidently rank one activity higher than the other as an exercise of intellect.)

Let it be said, furthermore, that commonplace assumptions about the vast difference between teacher and student are also under current challenge as inimical to effective learning and teaching communities. Flexibility about status is found desirable by universities that are moving toward combinations of discipline-oriented and life-reference studies. For while the status of the teacher is unambiguous on the discipline-oriented side, elsewhere it's a different story, with tricky subplots. (Social service is one activity; development of self or identity is another; exploring connections between disciplinary models and the edge of experience is another.) There's an emerging tendency to link rights and powers in academic government with activities rather than with formal titles, and to vary policy concerning admissions, grading and the like in accordance with the character of specific teaching and learning enterprises. Where a firm discipline is being introduced, by teachers who are competent to represent it, to students who freely elect it, the undergraduate claim to the right to hire and fire continues to be seen as weak. Where no discipline, or only the beginning of a discipline exists, and reliance on experiential perception is necessary, the undergraduate claim to that right—and to the right of self-evaluation—is held to be

stronger.* (Harvard's faculty accepted this principle when it granted students a full vote on
tenure appointments in its new black studies program.) The right would also be stronger in
programs where the focus is on social service or
on personal development than in programs where
the turn to experience is directed along carefully
judged disciplinary lines, and the student remains,
unambiguously, a student.

Given the variety of the challenges to ortho
doxy, the faculty statement might say, unqualified
endorsements of any single existing pedagogical
form conceivably could lock a university community into an unviable past. And, by the same
token, persistence in speaking as though the barrier between teacher and student must everywhere and always remain absolute can intensify
the difficulty of moving forward into a more
variegated teaching world. But at the same time
it *is* a fact that precisely because flexibility and
an atmosphere of hospitality to experiment in
teaching relationships are the order of the hour,
some members of the university are encouraged
to disruptive acts. They have violently interrupted discourse between students and teachers
and done dirt on the ideal of rational inquiry.
We call upon all members of the university community to stand firm against such behavior *without becoming stand-patters.* The search for new
terms of discourse and new forms of relatedness
in higher education is an intellectual venture; it
can't be pressed by mob action. Wherever it is

*Because all "courses" aren't courses. A good part of the con-
fusion about open admissions, for instance, stems from the pretense that all courses must be courses in the same sense, and that
grading the outcome of Multivariable Calculus is the same as grading the educational outcome of field experiences of the kind now
being supervised by social scientists in many urban universities. Professor Richard Mann at the University of Michigan runs an "Inner
City Course" requiring off-campus residence for six months in
Detroit, daily work in schools or day-care centers or welfare agencies,
as well as field study, readings and regular consultation with academic specialists. What could c-plus mean at the end of term here?

so pressed, we shall oppose it with all our force.
But our obligations can't be met merely by this
act of resistance. We must proceed with the
work of reconstituting teaching and learning
relationships through reasoned, collaborative
inquiry.

Ideally, a good law-and-order faculty document wouldn't stop here. It would go on to support its pieties about change, tolerance, openness
to new pedagogy, with practical recommenda-
tions, some clear next steps to be taken by university communities. It could speak up, for
instance, for an effort by student-faculty-admin-
istrator teams to identify teachers and advanced
students whose research or teaching suggests
sympathy with experientially-oriented pedagogy.
(The results of the inventory could be used to
shape proposals for restructuring in future years,
to determine policy concerning faculty recruit-
ment, and to guide thinking about the relative
amounts of student "time" to be spent in orthodox
courses and in a "school of immediate experience" in order to qualify for traditional degrees.*)
It could put an argument for an effort—by
another team—to identify opportunities in the
immediate environment (local government, business, agencies of welfare and of protest) for effective education, pointing outward from specific
disciplines toward life situations. It could pro-
pose that the same teams accept responsibility
for creating new agencies of communication
within their institution (instruments for circulating news about ventures in life-oriented educa-

*Some teachers, of course, teach "orthodox materials" in ways that
transform them, and the classroom itself, into immediate experience—
with no loss of intellectual rigor or balance. Prospects for the ultimate convergence of the traditional and the immediate, in the schools
of the future, depend largely on the success of graduate institutions
in rearing more teachers of this kind.

tion already in progress), and for preparing rationales for multi-track higher education (in anticipation of times when the work of acquainting alumni and the public with its intricacies and value could begin), and for developing lines of communication with private employers (for the purpose of educating them in the value and uses of experiential programs that may or may not lead to traditional degrees), and for starting conversations with graduate school admissions committees, looking first toward the creation of fresh ways of evaluating applicants and later toward the encouragment of multi-track graduate education. ("Student movements focusing much of their aggression on their undergraduate experience are really protesting practices which are traceable to shortcomings in the graduate schools," says Professor Richard Worthen, concluding a research-in-teaching project for the Carnegie Corporation that took him to hundreds of campuses. "In the long run a thoroughgoing reform of the graduate departments of our universities is just about as important as a solution to our current Vietnam dilemma.")

—All this is airy, I admit. I should also admit, no doubt, that the notions presented here aren't presented as disinterestedly as they should be. A few weeks back I had my first fall term moment of confrontation—a hassle with the Class Clan. A new course I was offering was over-enrolled—one hundred and thirty-six names had signed on for a "seminar" in contemporary American cultural studies (limited to twenty students). Say everything you can think of against the enrollees: Call them crazy mod-mad kids, abuse them for their boredom with the past, their lack of a sense of history, their absorption in NOW, etc. Still, they thought they wanted—these children—to do some contemporary cultural studies; they signed up. During the summer, several wrote letters pressing their claims. And most of them didn't get a shot at what they wanted. I made a small effort, I say defensively. Before the term began I called the registrar, a helpful, giving man. I suggested that, after filling a seminar for myself, I might send off a letter to the rejected, including a complete list of other enrollees and saying that if anyone wished to start a seminar on his own, with advice from me on possible assignments, and with an off-campus focus, he should write at once or see me in my office. (I had in mind some journalistic assignments the results of which could be played off against the work of newspaper professionals, as well as against Mailer, Wolfe and others, with an eye to clarifying and criticizing certain contemporary conventions of reportage.)

The answer was: Please bring up the question of credit. Your letter should specify "on a no-credit basis." The vote was definite last spring: A student-run political thing was turned down in faculty meeting . . . I could go see the dean . . . Best to move slowly . . . If they really want it, they'll do it anyway . . . No need for credit . . . A class is a class . . .

I admit this episode produced a patch of self-constriction and frustration and still colors my thoughts. I was itched by the stiffness that demanded absolute priority for the issue of credit. Up against the wall, kids. Frisk 'em, Mike. (Gotta watch these kids, they'll con you every time. . . .) Why couldn't we have started open and then closed in if they tried to con us? Why *begin* with a clanking gesture of suspicion?

But while this local exacerbation does stick in the memory, I wouldn't call it crucial. The arguments above are, after all, familiar, even commonplace; they don't need any particular person or situation to vouch for them. They amount at bottom to nothing more than a) a plea for faculty credibility, and b) a reiteration of the truism that academic freedom and obeisance to Standard-Current-Approved pedagogical forms aren't one and the same thing. The quite unradical (I think) assumption on which they rest is that while "we" have an obligation to protect each other's rights, we have a responsibility larger still—that of inventing an academic world consciously and explicitly adjusted to the huge variousness of the means by which men develop intellectual power and understanding. There are a hundred ways (mine are too crude and wordy: check) of building that assumption into a law-and-order document. And I'll sign and circulate, N., fight the good fight, the whole bit—I promise—once the assumption is built in.

But—apologies and thanks for the coffee—not until.

Is That Right, Mr. Yes?

By Michael Rossman

One of the learning games which is circulating
among the young on the campuses is "Totalitarian
Classroom," a game that relies on the degree to which
students (and teachers) have been blindly conditioned to play "good teacher/good student." T.C. is
a deconditioning device, and its players experience a
painful and illuminating perspective on the roles and
processes common to school and college classrooms.
The game, which bears family resemblance to
Brecht's theories about alienation in the theater, was
designed by Neil Kleinman, a young English professor at the University of Illinois who was deeply
involved with the study of modern theater. Like
many learning games, T.C. has spread quickly and
anonymously; among other places, it has been played
at Sonoma State, Denison, Antioch, Michigan, and
San Diego State, as well as at student conventions.

The game begins when its organizer announces to
a group of twelve to twenty innocents: "I want to
lead you in a learning game. Whoever plays must
observe a small set of rules and roles. These create
an artificial stage. Within it, let's try to have a real
discussion of how people act out their parts in
the classroom game called 'good student.' Maybe

we can extend the discussion to consider what the
'good student' game has to do with good learning,
if anything. The first rule assumes that everyone's
a 'good student'—independent, critical, with his own
unique viewpoint. So I'm always free to ask any
of you to express a view that differs from one just
given. You can extend it or contradict it. The second rule assumes that a 'good student' is in command of the material and can make connections between its parts. So I can call on anyone to explain
the connection between any two points other people
have previously made." (The organizer, of course,
need have no idea whether points are in fact con-
nectable: that's not his problem. He doesn't mention this, but goes on to ask for volunteers to play
three standard "good student" roles.) "One way to
present yourself as a 'good student' is to display your
command of the material. Another is to brown-nose,
to agree with the teacher. But you can also win
points by creative disagreement. So we'll want a
Scribe, to take absolutely verbatim notes. And a
Yes Man. When I ask—about anything—*Is that
right, Mr. Yes?* he replies, *Yes, that is right,* and
then explains why. Likewise we'll want a No Man,
whose job is to answer, when asked, *No, that is
wrong,* and then explain why. Is all this clear?"

"Are the rest of us supposed to play roles?"

"No. No one else should try to act a role. Everyone is free to respond as himself. Even the three
people who play Mr. Yes, Mr. No and Scribe should
respond as themselves except when I call on them
specifically in role. Let's try to keep the discussion as
real and substantive as we can."

Typically, the volunteers for Yes Man and No
Man depend on these strategies naturally. Often no
one will volunteer as Scribe. Insisting that verbatim
transcription is essential—which is true, since the
richest examples of "good student" performance lie

in the precise words people choose for their responses—the organizer drives the group into a
democratic election to burden someone with the job.
Later he pokes the Scribe with questions, illustrating
how impossible it is to think or respond while re-
cording material for playback. The discussion
begins. The organizer, no matter how gently or
jovially he may have introduced T.C., is in total
control. He is marked as the Expert, bankrolled
with specialized Knowledge, The Man Who Knows
What Should Happen. He uses the roles and rules
to punctuate or speed the game as well as to advance the discussion. They are the formal traces of
his control, which extends far beyond the stage
which the rules create for theater. With practice,
simply establishing their power is sufficient, and the
game may be run as desired with only rare recourse
to rules.

The game has three phases: In the first, by ask-
ing questions and giving hints, the organizer gets the
players to describe in detail the ways in which "good
students" act out their roles in the classroom theater:

"Very well, how do 'good students' project themselves?"

"They come to class on time."

"They hand in their homework."

"Yes, yes. Some others."

"Eye contact with the teacher is very important,
so is volunteering information."

"Seeing him after class to talk about something."

"What about the way people look? *You*—how
do you look when you've just been asked a question
you can't answer but you don't want the teacher to
know?"

"I sit up straight and wrinkle my forehead,
searching, maybe he'll speak first."

"And you?"

"I lean forward a little and look earnest, and try

to talk about something else."

"And you . . .?"

Soon the discussion reveals that the choices of where to sit, of posture, dress and expression, of complaisant or sarcastic attitude, are rich elements in a variety of ways of projecting oneself to teacher and class as a "good student." The organizer leads the group on, to recognize complete strategies:

"What might go with sitting in the back row and looking out the window to project a particular 'good student' image?"

"Missing a lot of classes but seeing the professor in his office, maybe not during regular hours."

"Being casual with your homework but sparkling on the final."

"You—what's the connection between the last two answers?"

"Both ways the student shows he knows what's important."

"Very good. This strategy will work with every teacher, is that right, Mr. No?"

"No, that's wrong."

"Because?"

"Because some teachers are uptight about petty detail."

"In other words, what's important is what *they* think is important. So it's clear different strategies work with different teachers and different classes. Now who can say why? What besides skill determines whether a projection of yourself as 'good student' will be successful?"

"If it helps the teacher play his own role well, if it complements his role."

"Is that right, Mr. Yes?"

"Yes, that's right, because then it satisfies his image of himself, it feeds his ego."

"Is that you or your role speaking?"

". . . Yes."

"Then does the image or role of a 'good student' necessarily resemble the image of the 'good teacher' he's facing?"

"No."

"Give an example—anyone."

"The class freak and the scholarly professor who translates the freak's occasional insights so the rest of the dull class can understand them."

"That'll do."

From the rhythms of an academic seminar, T.C. slips into Phase II—and reflects the theater in which the players, led by the organizer, comment on their own performance:

"How long do you think it takes to figure out what a teacher expects from you—which 'good student' roles will work with him?"

"Maybe like three weeks."

"Anyone think the time is shorter? You do— how short?"

"Oh, you can tell where most teachers are at in the first day or so."

"How? Tell *him* why it doesn't take three weeks."

"The way the teacher talks about midterms and homework, how he's dressed, whether he wants to bullshit a bit or get right down to the subject—things like that."

"Why did you look at me when you said that? I asked you to explain it to *him.*"

"I don't know."

"*You*—did that explanation make sense? Do you see why three weeks is too long?"

"Yes, I can see that the sizing-up starts right at the beginning, like whether the teacher asks the class questions about themselves."

"What is there in what he just said that presents *him* as 'good student'?"

"He admits his mistake."

"Anyone have a better answer?"

"He not only admits it, he shows he's learned by adding something new."

"Right on! Now go back. When I asked five of you how you looked when trying not to show you didn't know the answer to a question, everyone gave a different answer, which showed you're individuals —that's very good. But everyone answered in words. No one demonstrated the look itself, even though you know how many words a picture's worth. Why didn't you?"

"You wanted us to answer in words."

"How do you know? As a matter of fact, I was hoping someone wouldn't."

"I think it's because you're articulate."

"Why is *that* a 'good student' response?"

"He was uncertain and afraid you'd tell him he was wrong, so he took care to qualify it."

"Right. But I think he *is* right. How *does* my being articulate work?"

"What do you mean?"

"I mean the other side of the 'good student' game is the 'good teacher' game. In what ways have I been presenting myself as a 'good teacher' here?"

"Well, first, you stand at the front and you're always moving, so we have to focus on you. Second, you look people in the eye—that's how you call on them to speak, too. Third, you keep trying to probe deeper for answers. Fourth . . ."

"Stop. Anyone—how is *he* projecting himself as a 'good student'?"

"I'm *not* playing 'good student' . . ."

"I don't think you're trying to. Someone else answer."

"He volunteered."

"Something less trivial."

"He said, *first, second, third.*"

"Right! How is that a presentation of 'good student'?"

"It shows he has an orderly mind."

"Do you *always* say 'first, second, third'?"

"No."

"Why did you say it here? How did I cue that response?"

"*You* speak like that, even though you don't say the numbers."

"In what way was *that* a presentation as 'good student'?"

"He gave you a sharp answer, even though it might have displeased you personally."

"How do you know that strategy's a good one to

choose with me?"

"Because you wear your hair long."

While trying to keep the discussion unfolding, the organizer constantly calls attention to the way students act out the only roles they know how to assume in a context of directed learning. They cannot discuss the game without playing it. Pressure and pain mount. The players become confused and frustrated as they struggle with responses whose conditioned nature other players will eagerly and accurately point out. Asked, "Is that you speaking now or a role?" they often complain in anguish that they do not know. The group gives them no help. Although initially curious and open, the players are now withdrawn and angry. Sharp questions have goaded them through the leader's program of knowledge, making them feel stupid. Fellow members have vied to tear their answers down or give better ones. Reward has become to be left alone, punishment to be called on to answer. Only the Teacher's Pet is at east. (I have seen no one, however skilled, manage to avoid generating a Pet relationship with at least one player while directing T.C.: the conditioning runs deep.) The organizer's absolute control is further reaffirmed when he points out gently the violence he has been doing to individuals, their willingness to accept it, and the fact that few players have faced or addressed one another directly, and none have defended or supported another against attack. The players try to break past their role-confusion; the organizer co-opts any objection to the game, pushing the discussion on. The pressure soars until someone breaks—perhaps into tears, or by slamming out of the room. The organizer declares the game has ended, and asks the players to discuss the experience.

Phase III begins. In the second phase, the players, trapped in the game they were discussing, struggled with the pain of being unable to transcend their *individual* conditioning. In the final phase the agony continues. For although all have now agreed to stop playing the game, and perhaps have moved to another room, they find they are still playing the game *as a* group. They begin to discuss the experience in informal democracy, but when the organizer contributes his comments, the pattern of control reasserts itself. He no longer wants the role of Teacher and says so; but the group finds with dismay that it cannot treat him otherwise. He is still the Expert. All find that the context must be broken completely to permit a fresh start.

A full Totalitarian Classroom game takes about two hours. Well-run, it leaves its players shaken, acutely conscious of the game structure of classroom interaction, and of its destructive qualities. The players are also left with the realization that their performance as "good student" has little to do with *being* a good learner—a question which most realize they have rarely examined.

Malice in Wonderland
MISPERCEPTIONS OF THE ACADEMIC ELITE

By Andrew M. Greeley

It has been a bad summer for the academy. In a
recent Gallup Poll, the campuses found themselves described as the most serious problem the country faces,
bar none. They rank ahead of Vietnam, inflation and the
Black Panthers as a cause of national concern. The
academy has been appalled to discover that the majority
of Americans thought that the Kent State murders were
the fault of the students, and it has been amazed to learn
that its support for a political candidate could easily
become the kiss of death. Convinced as it was in the
spring, as indeed it has been these several springs past,
that it was the avant garde of a great popular revolution,
the academy now finds itself wondering about its very
survival, about the survival of its institutions, about the
survival of education itself. Characteristically, it blames
the situation on "the hard hats" or "the silent majority"
or "the fascist mass" and does not pause to ask whether
it is remotely possible that its own course has gone awry
somewhere in between.

A look back: in a great burst of social consciousness, the academy in the last five years has striven
passionately to be relevant. It has enlisted its students
from minority groups and turned a sensitive ear to the
aspirations of black and Third World peoples and to
students as a whole. It has turned its considerable energies to the remaking of society, in particular to the

causes of peace and racial justice. It would now appear that not merely have its efforts failed, but its efforts may even have become counterproductive to the very causes it has tried to support. Surely the academic peace movement, because of its tactics rather than its sentiments, has consistently hardened the stand of hawks in American society. It may very well turn out that academic support for the so-called black revolution has slowed down rather than accelerated the pace of social improvement for American Negroes. (The question poses itself whether the socio-political activity of the academy, whether the academy itself, is not being increasingly regarded by some as suspiciously un-American, given these prodigious results of its efforts.) Some of the more thoughtful academics who labored through the summer in the difficult task of trying to re-establish communication with the rest of American society are now trying to figure out what went wrong.

What exactly did go wrong? The root of the problem is that the "world outside" did not react the way it was supposed to react. Which is to say, the people who inhabit the world do not behave like academics. In this context, the word *academic* is not used to represent all, or even a majority of, college professors but rather the influential minority that sets the tone and the style and the fashion of the academy at a given time in its development. One must certainly include the allies of the academy in the mass media who tend to feel guilty vis-a-vis the full-fledged academic who presumably knows more and is morally purer than the huckster in the media. But the crisis in the relationship between the academy and the world outside is not simply that the academic does not understand the world outside, not even that he does not think it worthwhile to attempt to understand the world outside, but in fact that he is only barely aware that that world exists. The attitude was exquisitely summarized by a distinguished California political scientist at the time of Ronald Reagan's gubernatorial victory: "I'm astonished that the man won; nobody that I know voted for him."

The academic is so dazzled by the brilliance of his analysis and expression characterizing the world in which he lives that it is not at all difficult for him to ignore the existence of the rest of the world (save as the rest of the world is manifested in such social groups as the academic sees as special carriers of virtue—the youth and the blacks at the present time, for example).

Given the nature and the social functions of the academy, such unawareness is not surprising. The academic is expected to be deeply involved in his own teaching and research; the rest of the world not only tolerates but encourages his isolation because it has come to believe that the isolation is necessary for the academic to do whatever he is supposed to do. Whether the isolation is ever really desirable may be a matter for question but it creates no serious problems until the academic discovers, usually with an overwhelming sense of guilt, that there are many things wrong with the rest of the world. Looking around and discovering the injustice and immorality "outside," he righteously decides something must be done about it. He asks, "If something must be done, then who better to do it?"

Perhaps the best possible answer to that question is, "Just about anyone." For when the academy decides to remake the rest of the world, whether the world wants to be remade or not, there is likely to be trouble, if only because the academic is but dimly aware of what motivates those human beings who are to be the object of his missionary zeal.

There are assumptions underlying such academic zealotry: 1) the academy knows how to remake society; 2) the rest of society will fall into line and permit itself to be remade once the academy has pointed out the nature of its immorality; and 3) the rest of society will be willing to pick up the tab while the academy proceeds to shape society according to its own image and likeness.

But none of these assumptions has proven true. Those who resist the academy's missionary zeal can point out that the academics have an extremely difficult time keeping their own house in order, that the academic departments in colleges are usually but one step removed from chaos, that there is little evidence that the academy has been very successful in its primary task of educating the young, and that it resolutely resists attempts by "outsiders" to evaluate its performance. In other words, the academy, having been unsuccessful in its own function, now assumes that it should be permitted to appropriate the functions of a number of other social institutions. Having failed to run the university well, it now assumes the right to be permitted to run the rest of society.

Such blithe academic pretensions are hardly justified by the realities. The facile talk around the universities about a coalition made up of "the young, the black, the poor, and the disaffected professionals" ignores the fact that the academy can count on the support of, at the most, one-third of the young, one-fifth of the black, and one-tenth of the whole country. Eldridge Cleaver and Leroi Jones speak no more for the silent majority of American blacks than Rennie Davis, Tom Hayden and Abbie Hoffman speak for more than a tiny fraction of those young people who have attended college. In fact, George Wallace seems to speak for more of the young nationwide than he does for adults.

In her book *On Violence,* Hannah Arendt, with characteristically incisive style, dismisses "the third world coalition" version of the academic assumption.

> The students caught between the two superpowers and equally disillusioned by East and West "inevitably pursue some third ideology, from Mao's China or Castro's Cuba." Their calls for Mao, Castro, Che Guevara, and Ho Chi Minh are like pseudo-religious incantations for saviors from another world; they would also call for Tito if only Yugoslavia were farther away and less approachable. The case is different with the Black Power movement; its ideological commitment to the non-existent "Unity of the Third World" is not sheer romantic nonsense. They have an obvious interest in a black-white dichotomy; this too is of course mere escapism—an escape into a dream world in which Negroes would constitute an overwhelming majority of the world's population.

Miss Arendt also disposes neatly of the third academic assumption—the assumption that society will sit idly by and allow itself to be remade.

Self-interest, when asked to yield to "true" interest—
that is, the interest of the world as distinguished from
that of the self—will always reply, Near is my shirt,
nearer is my skin. That may not be particularly reasonable, but it is quite realistic; it is the not very noble
but adequate response to the time discrepancy between men's private lives and the altogether different
life expectancy of the public world. To expect people,
who have not the slightest notion of what *res publica*,
the public thing, is, to behave nonviolently and argue
rationally in matters of interest is neither realistic nor
reasonable.

To put the whole matter more directly, the academy is not the place to develop the skills required for
political action, for persuasion, for coalition formation,
for development of consensus; indeed, the academy is
not even the place where most men can expect to
acquire the skills which are necessary for dealing respect-
fully with those who have the temerity to exist beyond
the boundaries of the academic grove.

To the world outside, the academic missionary looks
intolerant, reactionary, authoritarian, hypnotized by his
own rhetoric, and ignorant of political reality. When
such a man becomes involved in politics, the first reaction of the world outside is to laugh; its second,
perhaps, to call a psychiatrist; and its third, as it turns
out, to summon the police or the National Guard.

The accusation of intolerance is especially hard for
the academy to bear because it has always prided itself
on its openness and ability to accept deviance and dissent. Yet Professor Marcuse's philosophical intolerance
quickly found a hearing in academia, and for the past
five years the academy has sat on its hands while young
fascist toughs have disrupted other people's right of
freedom of speech and freedom of assembly. Nor does it
have much room for those who dissent in other than the
fashionable and approved mode. The cases of W.W. Rostow, Arthur Jensen, and Daniel Patrick Moynihan each
illustrate how little room there is in the academy for
dissent that is not approved by the arbiters of fashion. I

happen to disagree with Rostow and Jensen, and to agree with Moynihan. The issue is not the personalities or the beliefs of the three but whether the intellectual positions they take are to be the objects of rational and civilized discussion. The fashion of self-righteous dismissal of their positions prior to such discussion is as classic a case of intolerance as one could ask for.

Rostow and Jensen have been effectively punished and apparently even reduced to silence, though a very distinguished American scholar displayed what I take to be an authentically tolerant reaction to Jensen. When asked whether he thought that Jensen was a racist or not, the scholar replied, "What does it matter?" There was a time when such a response in the academy would have been taken for granted. Moynihan, cut from a somewhat different cloth, has chosen to fight back [see the introduction to the new edition of *Beyond the Melting Pot*]. But one is not surprised, not at least if one knows academia from the inside, by the intolerance displayed toward these men. One need only to read the book reviews and the letters to the editor in professional journals or to participate in the factional feuds which yearly rack academic departments to know that in academia certain kinds of dissent are legitimate and others strictly off the mark. The academic is serenely confident of his own judgment and thus assumes that those who dare to disagree with him are not only wrong but are either stupid or in bad faith or, quite conceivably, both. It is amusing to read the words of a card-carrying academic like Columbia historian Robert Paul Wolff, in his *Ideal of the University* (see also *Change*, September-October 1969). He engages in some embarrassingly painful anti-Catholic bigotry—of the sort that one had thought academics had long ago given up—and trots out the hoary cliche about the similarity between loyalty to Rome and loyalty to Peking and Moscow. Wolff is exceedingly confident, of course, that he is himself undoctrinaire and undogmatic, even though he has jointly authored a collection of essays with Professor Marcuse and has written in his *Ideal of the University* what is almost a caricature of academic dogmatism.

One of the quaint notions of the academy is that

certain groups of people are what we used to call in
Christianity "confirmed in grace"—which is to say that
they can do no wrong and that any attempt to bring
them to trial for alleged wrongdoing is "political perse-
cution." Thus, Father Berrigan was described as the first
priest to be a political fugitive, even though there are
many clergymen who held exactly the same positions
but were not fugitives because they had not destroyed
government property. Similarly, it would appear that
many in the Yale community believe that it is immoral
to bring the Black Panthers into court no matter how
strong the evidence or how brutal the crime. Any charges against the Panthers are by definition political, in
their view. Tom Hayden did little more than reflect the
attitude of many in the Yale community when he announced that in this case the facts were completely
irrelevant. Surely this is a rather quaint notion of justice,
one with which the family of the young black who was
killed might, with good reason, disagree.

If academics cannot be·tolerant of those who dissent within their own grove, it is hardly likely that they
will be tolerant enough to engage in persuasion instead
of denunciation when they venture beyond their own
boundaries. Nor, for all their claims to be "liberal" or
"radical," are academics inclined to be either liberal or
radical when their own self-interests are at stake. They
are only too happy to be liberal or radical with the jobs
of construction workers, the schools of white ethnics,
the admission standards for other peoples' children; but
when it comes to their own course schedule, their own
class hour loads, the requirements in their own departments, the sanctity of their own teaching style, or the
privileges of their own classrooms, academics yield to no
one in their ability to resist change and progress. Anyone
who is engaged in educational reform efforts (which do
not involve closing down class and sending faculty and
students off to the barricades) realizes that the real
barrier to educational reform is the faculty. It is at
precisely those schools where the faculty has the greatest
power that instructional change is the least likely to
occur. The suggestion of Wolff and others that the
college be turned over to the faculty (and their student

allies) would guarantee absolute paralysis of all efforts at instructional reform. He who is not open to change in his own bailiwick demands change from others with very little grace. And the world outside can say to the academic, "Why do you presume to demand that we make sacrifices, when you're not willing to give up anything yourself?"

So convinced is he of the need of virtue—and of course of his own virtue—that the academic is perfectly willing to impose virtue on others, so long as it is his kind of virtue. The faults and the failings of the Grand Inquisitor are railed against in the literature courses, but they have not by any means been exorcised from the academy. The latest scheme for imposing virtue is the "randomization of admissions" advocated by Wolff and others. The splendid plurality and pluralism of higher education is to be abolished. Students are no longer to choose their own college, and colleges are no longer to choose their own students. The great god of the computer will randomly assign students to institutions, and they will have to go there whether they want to or not. It will, of course, take an immense amount of coercion —either governmental or quasi-governmental—to impose such a "noble experiment," and a vast amount of supervision and enforcement machinery to make sure there are no violations.

Young people would be inclined to despise the school they were being forced to attend, and faculty members would find it difficult to teach students who were in a school they did not want to attend. Parents might rebel at paying for an education in an institution in which they had no confidence. But these kinds of reactions from free men demanding freedom of choice are to be casually dismissed in the name of "equality of opportunity." De Tocqueville feared that America would be a country where freedom would be sacrificed in the name of equality. From the point of view of authoritarians like Wolff, this has turned out to be a happy prediction.

There is, of course, no evidence that such randomization of admissions would indeed do much to facilitate the equality of opportunity in American society, just as

there is no evidence that compulsory busing of white
students to black schools does much to improve educational opportunities for black students. However, both
procedures are immensely satisfying to the academic
turned philosopher-king and his need for order, neatness
and virtue. The whole question of equality of opportunity is a complex one that is beyond the scope of this
essay, but it is sufficient to say that it is not a problem
that will yield to simpleminded solutions, even when
these solutions are not such as to require that they be
imposed on the rest of society with brute force.

Wolff is in favor of randomization of admissions
more because it will eliminate the horror of taking
college entrance exams for young people than because it
will equalize the social structure. I do not like the
"college boards" because I don't think they evaluate
anything meaningful; and I think the emotional atmosphere around them usually engendered by upper-
middle-class parents—is sick. But in a society such as
ours there is going to be at some point an "objective"
evaluation of competency, and Wolff's reform will not
eliminate it. His solution would mean that the anxiety
would focus on the toss of the dice rather than on
something over which a young person has some control.
Postponing that evaluation would create new problems.

The academic is convinced in his heart of hearts that
those on the outside are not virtuous, because of ignorance or malice or both; therefore, he sees no choice but
to constrain them to virtue. It is but one logical step,
then, to argue, as a sociologist recently argued in *The
New York Times Magazine,* that since one cannot get
virtuous action by majority rule, one must abandon
majority rule; and it is but one more logical step to
sympathize with, and even applaud, violence as a means
of forcing society to be virtuous. When a minority im-
poses its will on the majority, especially by violence,
what one has, of course, is fascism. The tragic young
SDS leader who was destroyed by one of his own bombs
really made explicit what he had learned from his men-
tors when he commented that if fascism was what was
required, then fascism it would be. One ought not to be
surprised if the rest of society chooses to call the Na-

tional Guard when faced with a minority dedicated to imposing its own notion of virtue on the majority.

What is missing from the academic's morality is the capacity for compassion—at least compassion for those who are not members of the groups that have been deemed acceptable recipients of compassion. The Yale faculty member whom Michael Lerner quotes as implying that Italians are an inferior race (because Mario Procaccino dared to run against the WASP saint, John Lindsay) is not the sort of man one wants to see engaging in political behavior.

Kenneth Keniston has argued repeatedly that many student radicals are young men and women of very high moral development, but recently he has had some doubts about abstract moral principles. They are, he suggests in an article in *Youth and Society* (September 1969) :

> . . .intimately—perhaps inevitably—related to the development of moral self-righteousness, zealotry, dogmatism, fanaticism, and insensitivity . . . In pursuit of his own personal principles, a man will ride rough-shod over others who do not share these principles, will disregard human feelings, or even destroy human life. During the period when the "end of ideology" was being announced on all sides, when instrumental and consensus politics were being extolled, we learned to identify abstract personal principles with dogmatic and destructive moral zealotry. How are we to combine these two perspectives? Do we see in Brewster Smith's findings confirmation of the view that student activists are dangerous moral zealots? Or do we adhere to Kohlberg's implication that such individuals are more likely moral heroes than despots?

Keniston's response is that "whether the highest stages of moral reasoning lead to destructive zealotry or real ethicality depends upon the extent to which moral development is *matched by development in other sectors*. The critical related sectors of development, I submit, are those which involve compassion, love, or empathic identification with others." Keniston goes on to say:

> Many moral zealots, bigots, and dogmatists are of course describable, in Kohlberg's terms, as conventionalists, while others are perhaps permanent regressees to the Raskolnikoff Syndrome. But there are at least a

few whom we know from personal experience or from history who seem truly post-conventional in moral reasoning, but whose genuine adherence to the highest moral values is *not* matched by compassion, sympathy, capacity for love and empathy. In such individuals, the danger of breaking human eggs to make a moral omelet, of injuring people in order to advance one's own moral principles, is all too real (Laqueur, 1962). Thus, neatly to identify even the highest levels of moral reasoning with human virtue, much less with mental health, maturity, and so on, would be a serious mistake. What we might term "moral precocity" in youth—high moral development not attended by comparable development in other sectors of life—may indeed be dangerous. . . . What is dangerous is any level of moral development, be it post-conventional, conventional, or pre-conventional, in the absence of a developed capacity for compassion, empathy and love for one's fellow men.

All of which is surely very true, and anyone who knows Professor Keniston knows that he is personally a superb example of compassion, love and empathy. But what is one to say of an alleged pattern of moral development which produces principles without necessarily producing compassion, love or empathetic identification? Professor Keniston himself admits:

. . . what is true for most is not true for all, and historically, many crimes have been committed in the name of the highest principles, sincerely held. In the end, the findings of developmental psychology in the context of youthful political activism may merely return us to ancient truisms—compassion without morality is sentimental and effusive, while morality without compassion is cold and inhumane.

Indeed, yes, one is forced to say, but then compassion is at the very core of morality. The moral system which does not demand compassion is an inadequate moral system. But one wonders why the academy is discovering compassion so very late in the radical game.

The academic is skilled in the articulation of his thought. In his ordinary activity of teaching and research such skills are of immense value, but they can be counterproductive when he chooses to engage in political rhetoric. Unlike the politician, the academic seems to be subject to the temptation to take his rhetoric not only seriously but literally. If he speaks of *revolution*, he actually begins to believe that there is a revolution. If he tosses around the word *establishment* a sufficient number of times, he begins to believe that it is not a mythological term but one to which there is a corresponding reality. If he pontificates often enough about what the "young" and the "black" want, then he will begin to believe that the few young people he knows and the few blacks he has heard or read actually represent what the majority of the young and the black are really seeking. If he compares the United States frequently enough to Nazi Germany, he begins to believe that there are Nazi stormtroopers in the streets, that Richard Nixon actually is an Adolf Hitler who intends to cancel the 1972 election, that John Mitchell really is a Heinrich Himmler who is setting up concentration camps, that the United States has really embarked on a policy of genocide against the black and brown people in its midst, and that Daniel Berrigan, in a mad exercise of romantic narcissism, has become Dietrich Bonhoeffer reincarnate.

This confusion of rhetoric with reality involves no particular problem unless one chooses one's political strategy to fit one's rhetoric. If one really believes that he is in a Nazi society and that there is a revolution in progress, then he is not likely to attempt to engage in political dialogue with the 90 percent of the society that has sold out to the Nazis.

And yet, it is a peculiar kind of revolutionary rhetoric. Secure in his tenured professorship in the department of semantics at the Massachusetts Institute of Technology, Professor Noam Chomsky can call other scholars mandarins. Theodore Roszak, in a very scholarly, mass-produced paperback volume, can denounce both objective conciousness and technology, which apparently means other people's objective consciousness and other people's technology. University faculties, one of the most secure and established groups in our society, see no contradiction in denouncing the "establishment" and are utterly horrified when the rest of society threatens to hack at the university's budgetary increase for the

next academic year. One wonders in passing what kind of revolution it is when the revolutionaries expect to collect their salaries or their grade point averages while continuing to engage in their revolutionary activities. One wonders if there was a single faculty member in the country who lost a single day's pay during the so-called May Revolution. The academic is so bemused by his own rhetoric that he thinks he can keep on biting the hand that feeds him without that hand ever becoming so "immoral" as to withdraw itself.

Finally, from the point of view of the world outside, academics, when they begin to engage in social reform, show extraordinary ignorance. Arnold Kaufman, the philosopher, recently admitted that he and a number of other California academics made a mistake when they argued four years ago that there was no difference between Pat Brown and Ronald Reagan. Men who are so tardy in coming to so obvious a conclusion can scarcely expect to be taken very seriously, but the academic-turned-social-reformer is simply not aware of how other people think or feel. He can write them off as hard hats, or white ethnics, or middle Americans; he can dismiss them as admirers of Mayor Daley, and that settles the problem. That they might be deeply, even passionately concerned about their neighborhood, about their schools, about safety in the streets, about patriotic values, about morality, and about religion is of no consequence to the academic except as evidence of how benighted and inferior these "hard hats" really are. Are they put off by beards, long hair, drugs, free sex and bizarre clothes? Well then, so much the worse for them; as one professor observed in *The New York Times Magazine*, "No reasonable man could object to someone wearing a beard." The 90 percent who constitute the "hard hat" society are then not reasonable men and are not to be taken seriously; but even though they are not reasonable, it is still expected that they will continue to finance the subversion of their own value system and their own social structure by those who have dismissed them as unreasonable.

So dogmatically convinced are the academic reformers of the rightness of their own analysis that they are quite unaware of the almost total failure of direct action protests since 1967. They are also convinced that student enthusiasm was responsible for Senator McCarthy's early primary victories, and that the confrontation between Mayor Daley's police and the student radicals in front of Chicago's Conrad Hilton Hotel was what beat Hubert Humphrey. The existence of impeccable research demonstrating that the students had little impact on the early support for Senator McCarthy and that the battle of Chicago was, if anything, an asset to the Democratic party is not likely to change their opinion. One is reminded again of the political scientist who did not know anyone who voted for Ronald Reagan.

So convinced is the academic of the superiority of his own position that he is certain that the petitions he signs, the resolutions he votes for, and the interminable discussions in his faculty meetings will have an automatic importance in the world beyond the academic groves. And when he moves out of the grove, not merely to remake society, but to engage in direct political campaigning, he does so with the serene confidence that his political activity could not possibly turn out to be counterproductive. It is absolutely unthinkable, for example, that other voters may be incensed and even infuriated if universities close down two weeks before the election and hordes of young people swarm about the country as political missionaries. The hard hat who must continue on his job is supposed to take it for granted that the morally superior academic is exempt from any equal obligation.

The typical academic suffers from an excess of what can only be called religious zeal and a deficiency of sensitivity to the hopes and fears of those different from himself. These characteristics may not be an accident. Sociological research by Joseph Zelan and myself indicates that academics are disproportionately recruited from those who come from unhappy families, have left behind their own religious faith, and have turned to academia as a substitute church. Furthermore, the graduate school training process is the logical conclusion to an educational system which trains one to develop as fully as possible his capacity for abstract cognition and articulation at the expense of his poetic, intuitive, and imaginative capacity. Emotions are socially approved in academia as long as one is able to talk about them rationally and articulately. Thus, Roszak and other advocates of the counterculture (who incidentally make the marvelous assumption that the counterculture could survive even if it weren't subsidized by the main culture) sing the glories of feeling and emotion when enjoyed by those who are objective and articulate. The poor slobs who are incapable of that kind of self-analysis are of course "hard hats," and neither they nor their emotions are to be taken very seriously.

If one looks for historical analogies to the combination of limited cognition and religious fervor that cause individuals to embark on the path of political and social reform, one must turn to the Middle Ages and those peculiar institutions, the religious-military orders. The Knights Templar, the Knights of St. John, the Teutonic Knights, venturing forth into battle with bravery, zeal,

and fervor, were very much like today's academic cru-
sader-reformers, with one difference: the crusader-knights in the Middle Ages won some signal victories (one order, the Knights of Malta, has managed to
survive to the present day, though they are not presently
fighting any crusade). The "crusader-knights" of the
contemporary academy, however, are not winning any
victories, and, in some instances, they are even snatching
defeat from the jaws of victory. It would be much
better, one suspects, if they went back to teaching
students or, to be precise, if they *began* to teach students.

Yet one need not despair completely. Many of the
faculty and students who are preparing to engage in the
fall political campaigns are approaching their work as
dialogists and not as missionaries. They seem to be
willing not only to talk to potential converts in the silent
majority but also to listen to them – a difficult task for
anyone, and especially for an intellectual. A small but
growing group of young people – one thinks particularly
of Michael Lerner and Wallace Roberts – have already
discovered that it is possible for a young liberal academic
to learn something from a middle-aged ethnic working
man. If the fall campaign produces more young
academics who are tolerant of and compassionate
toward those who are different from them, it might be a
revolution of considerable importance in American
social relationships. It might even be that a new
generation of academics will emerge who do not see
their vocation as compelling them to destroy and remake
their students' values. Under such circumstances, real
higher education – which necessarily respects who the
students are and where they come from – might begin.

The Business of "Business as Usual"

by David Riesman

The events of Cambodia, followed by the killings of students at Kent State and Jackson State, have for some of us rendered "business as usual" an almost unthinkable prospect. These cataclysmic events have had perhaps their greatest impact on the previously apathetic on already partly politicized campuses. The apathetic have a way of being stampeded, precisely because they have not been paying attention in the past. Their views tend not to be anchored by anything but the shallowest of convictions. This can make them dangerous, once aroused and galvanized. And faculty members, suddenly discovering a crisis that has in fact been around for a long time, can carry the weight of their scholarly authority into territories where their knowledge and perceptions are exceedingly limited.

In times of great national crisis it may be necessary to drop everything. But the Cambodian crisis of May was, in my opinion, principally a dramatic revelation of the inherent danger of the policy of Vietnamization, with its built-in danger of possible or alleged Dunkirks and of reescalation: it was not a sudden or new danger. The attack on "business as usual" emanates chiefly from the newly enraged and engaged faculty, and less from those of us who have been in the role of Cassandra over the years. Even in May 1970 it was probably true that most students and faculty interrupted their lives only temporarily, if at all, out of concern for the war or for other social catastrophes. And even in the more feverish avant garde universities, there remained areas of undistracted work and undiluted leisure.

Nevertheless, in many liberal arts colleges, what began as the attack by tiny minorities against mindless routines has now become sufficiently effective to create at least a temporary addiction to emergencies and to the emotional camaraderie these engender at their outset. It is in such institutions that it becomes especially necessary to understand the implications of attacking business as usual and of devoting the energies of faculty and students to a single cause, no matter how compelling.

The scorn for business as usual is often an implicit attack on businessmen, made by people who regard their own occupation or source of income as somehow more pure. More generally, it is an attack on routine as such, on the usual, on the non-dramatic and ordinary work of life. There may also be the implicit insistence that, as we do not live in normal times, the effort to lead a balanced or judicious life is somehow morally reprobate and not consonant with our epoch.

Many of our students, however, have few or no established routines. They have discarded the alarm clock and the schedule as inhibiting to impulse and spontaneity. They have not lived long enough to experience alterations of routine and urgency linked to national events and private dramas. Students seldom have experience with the complex relations between work and its consequences. They may even assume that the atmosphere of a revival meeting is conducive to serious political work, and they are not prepared for the backsliding, exhaustion and despair that often follow such meetings, at least when immediate results are not forthcoming. Lulled by notions of technical abundance, many students and faculty members take it for granted that other people will go on doing their work as usual, and that they themselves need feel no responsibility for this. Business as usual is in fact something of a

continuing achievement, and we need it in order to perform
the unusual. The anti-Vietnam war activities in which many
of us have been involved in recent years would not have
been possible if the telephone operators had not done their
business as usual, or the secretaries, or the airlines.

I n our role as educators, we faculty members need to
consider the lessons students draw from the way we handle
our own commitments. We need to demonstrate that it is
possible to think about more than one thing at a time, to
attend to our classes and to problems of university "business," while also involving ourselves as citizens in political
and cultural life. Especially on those campuses or in those
departments where the politically committed have moral
hegemony, faculty members need to support the position
of those students who go about their business of learning
and not allow them to be browbeaten as being merely
selfish. Indeed, many students, like many faculty, have
been able to involve themselves simultaneously or in rapidly
alternating cycles in political and in academic work. Thus,
students who worked in the early sixties for a moratorium
on nuclear testing did not ask for a moratorium on
examinations.

Even in short-run tactical terms, the universities are
only of modest and perhaps self-defeating use as institutional bases for the anti-war movement. Of course, the
colleges can facilitate the anti-war work of individual
students, faculty members and organized groups by collect-
ing them in a single place and by drawing on the understanding of issues gained through research and scholarship.
Hard as it is to draw the line in either theory or practice,
however, universities as institutions should not be committed by their members to a single position on the war or
other issues.

To destroy the ability of universities to shelter more
than one passionate conviction at a time does not help even
that one conviction, for our problems will not yield to the

instant outcry of the educated, or even to a single summer's campaigning. A competent psychoanalyst can sometimes help an individual change himself over the course of many months of intensive work. Can it be easier to change the course of a whole society?

In a world of armed and competing nationalisms, it is vital to survival to have enclaves which can free a few individuals to rise above mass and class passions. In a society more stratified and aristocratic than ours, some members of the nobility may be removed from the nationalism of the general population by their international connections. In the United States, in the absence of a genuine establishment, the modest autonomy and detachment of the universities are needed as protection against ourselves. They need to preserve their pluralism, their willingness to harbor men of many causes and commitments, their refusal to commit themselves as institutions to any single position. This is so even when the cause in question is internationalist, or indeed, for the moment, anti-American.

This country was subject to the fevers of jingoism long before the rise of contemporary mass media. These media, however, make the situation of the country ever more precarious, so that our society sometimes appears like a ferry boat with a great many passengers who rush madly first to one side, tipping the boat until it nearly keels over, and then to the other side, tipping it the other way. Radio and television have reduced the distances in space and time which once could buffer the impact of news and its interpretation. Everyone, at least in the university world, knew instantly about the Kent State, Augusta and Jackson State killings. And that knowledge in the absence of instantaneous remedy may perhaps have increased our sense of helplessness, although it is doubtful whether we are in fact more helpless than when we knew less of what was going on, or heard of it more slowly.

When the Japanese struck Pearl Harbor, radio carried the news at once, and for many in the general population there was an immediate response that the United States must strike back at the Japanese; there was no national disagreement. Franklin Roosevelt allowed that he was no longer going to be Dr. New Deal, but henceforth Dr. Win the War. It pleased him to be able to abandon the complexities of intricate domestic issues to the apparent simplicities of combat. Domestically, the war spirit encouraged West Coast and military racists to treat the Nisei as enemies and to evacuate them to concentration camps. In foreign affairs, we were tempted to fight a military rather than a political war. We demanded Unconditional Surrender from our enemies in part because the Russians feared a separate peace, but in part because of the vindictiveness let loose against the Japanese people, and also against all Germans, who were labeled as Nazis and Huns without discrimination. This doctrine of Unconditional Surrender forced many Germans, who might have preferred otherwise, to stay with the Nazi leadership. We solidified the hold of enemy leadership by dropping incendiary and destructive bombs on the civilian populations of

cities such as Hamburg, Dresden and Tokyo (much as we have done in North Vietnam and, indeed, in South Vietnam), and we did so with almost no domestic criticism. And we dropped atomic bombs, first on Hiroshima and then on Nagasaki, at a time when the Emperor and his circle (protected by their elite position from the blind fanaticism of many army men) were already making desperate efforts to surrender. Pearl Harbor silenced the criticism of former isolationists, and indeed brought many of them into a passionate mood of uncritical interventionism. Our universities were less influential then than now, but they did little to resist the tendency to think only of one enemy at a time, one goal at a time, one idea at a time.*

It may be that the soldier in battle needs to think obsessively about only one thing at a time in order to survive, although studies of the morale of armies suggest that unit loyalty may be more important than hatred of the enemy. Our generals, however, have often seemed to me to play a kind of one-man chess, thinking only of what they can do to the enemy and not of what the enemy can do in return, or of the social consequences for us of what we do to the enemy. We are all aware of the senior military men (and, no less important, the many civilians) who have believed from the outset that the problem in Vietnam was to win the war and get it over with, even if it meant the destruction of an entire country. Such men, remote from battle, should be able to consider the question whether it is good for a country or for an individual in this shrinking and over-amplified world to win all the battles.

However, a similar one-man chess is often played by students and faculty who are dragging the universities along

*I recognize that writers such as Gar Alperovitz maintain that we did fight a political war, and that the atomic bomb was dropped in large measure to intimidate Stalin rather than to force the Japanese to a surrender which in the end became conditional, since the Emperor was kept. The text must stand as shorthand for a concededly controversial position on issues that I regard as still tangled in historical uncertainty.

with them in crusades against war, imperialism or racism.
They may sometimes intentionally disregard what the
domestic backlash can do to them. But at other times they
approach the possibility of domestic success with political
demands that amount to Unconditional Surrender; one
often hears students say that they have given The System
a chance (as in the Eugene McCarthy campaign or in various
demonstrations), and it didn't respond, and so they have
turned to despair—or to violence. What this impatience
suggests is something that is very American. Even those
who regard themselves proudly as nonconformists share the
general American impatience with what is thought of as evil
or incompetence; and there is always the temptation
toward anarchic individualism, even when we act under
slogans of love and amity.

Of course, there are differences among Americans in
what might be termed opinion-proneness: the educated are
more likely than the less educated to have opinions and to
react quickly to events; the urban more likely than the
rural; and the well off, with time to spare, more likely than
those struggling for subsistence. While part of the population can be moved to thoughtless activism by the attrac-
tions of bellicosity, our noblest emotions can also be
exploited in the service of onesidedness; here I think of the
way in which guilt for racial oppression or for apathy or
privilege can sometimes be exploited. The lability of educated and generous opinion makes it all the more necessary
for universities to remain as a place of recourse for
individuals engaged with issues that are not at the moment
fashionable, or, in the current temper, even urgent. The
universities are a place to store the seed corn of ideas
against famines that may last a long time and take unex-
pected forms.

What happened in some of the major universities at
the height of the civil rights movement in the early sixties is
an example of being swept up by a cause and thinking only

of one thing at a time. It seemed to me then that most of my politically alert friends and students were thinking only of one issue at a time—namely, the race question. After the Cuban Missile Crisis and the 1963 Test Ban, the atomic explosion at Alamogordo dropped pretty much out of their consciousness (I am less sure about the unconscious). During that period, most of the university people I knew were extremely inattentive to Vietnam. (As late as the 1968 election campaigns, few of even the most informed people seemed aware that Vice President Richard Nixon, along with Admiral Arthur Radford, wanted to come to the aid of the French with atomic weapons at Dienbienphu in 1954.) For many academic people, only the escalations of 1965 brought them out of their involvement with domestic issues and helped them focus on Vietnam.

No society and no university can afford to have only a single focus of attention. Many of us can foresee a new provincialism setting in if we ever manage to extricate ourselves from Southeast Asia. (When I encounter attacks on college language requirements, I have sometimes argued in favor of language-immersion programs which would truly put students into another culture—only to find these rejected on the ground that America's pressing domestic problems should engage every single one of us, not merely most of us.)

To be sure, there is a small number of students and faculty who interpret events in Southeast Asia in the light of a general theory of American or Western imperialism and racism. They are likely to continue their concern with the impact of America on the rest of the world, cultural and political when no longer military. It is important to have such positions represented in the universities, whatever one may think about their accuracy. For it is the job of universities to be sure that there are people around who state problems in various ways, and who have other priorities as well as the prevalent ones. But for this to happen, the universities must prevent any single group from forcing its particular tone and agendas either on its own members or on the rest of us in an all-encompassing way. We need to have available to us the possibility of understanding other times, other societies, other periods of stress.

I myself have believed since Hiroshima that mankind now does face a novel danger of total extinction. But if I thought only about that and did not go on some of the time with my business and life as usual, I do not think I could do anything useful about the nuclear threat or about anything else. Since it is quite possible and even likely that life may go on, and conceivable that we can learn to control the atom and other weapons of mass destruction, we need to live at this moment as if there will be more moments to come. We need to resist now fashionable seductions of despair no less than the earlier comforts of complacency.

The Revolt Against Democracy

By Edgar Z. Friedenberg

There is a widespread conviction among dissenting youth today that they are oppressed by a fundamentally illegitimate authority. For the younger members of a gerontocracy like ours to regard the authority of the older generation as oppressive is a rational act; that such authority should be logically regarded as oppressive is implicit in the fact that it occasions revolt. But for authority to be regarded likewise as illegitimate is something new. It makes conflict far more disruptive. It is, in fact, the characteristic that most clearly distinguishes today's intergenerational conflict from that which commonly occurs between successive generations.

Legitimacy is the chief lubricant of the social mechanism; it prevents friction by inducing collaboration among its several parts even in situations in which conflict of interest is apparent. The extreme example is the quiet dignity with which the condemned so often cooperate with their executioners. In the ultimately terrifying situation, the victim takes what comfort he can from identifying himself as a member of the society which has officially certified him as so worthless that he must be publicly destroyed. By so doing, he is not alone in his moment of mortal terror.

In a social system that has exhausted its legitimate authority, however, executions are regarded as publicly planned assassinations that invite resistance, escalation and, ultimately, role-confusion, as Danton and Robespierre discovered. Declining legitimacy leads to a rise in coercive violence, which is usually attributed to the disorderly provocation of those who have no respect for "authority" or "law and order." Analysis of the actual events more often discloses that the contrary is true: violence is launched and maintained by terrified officials who feel their authority threatened. As their legitimacy ebbs, they fall back on the resources for coercion which their official position affords, and modern technology has made these resources enormous. Whether this results in the re-establishment of legitimacy depends on whether a stable regime can be built on the wastelands of terror. In the past it has usually been possible, but it does take time—more than a generation.

Terror thus is not a very useful device for restoring the faith of the younger generation in the legitimacy of the authority of their elders. Indeed, the authorities in this country have so structured their recent confrontations with the young as to reveal their own cognizance of the illegitimacy of their authority. This is the era of *plainclothes* police cracking the skulls of students, of *undercover* narcotics agents busting students for smoking pot. A uniform is an asset to the officer of a society whose legitimacy is accepted; the uniform, as with the soldier, legitimates even lethal hostility, if there is any legitimacy left. But out of uniform the adversary is a spy, and he himself becomes the legitimate object of condemnation. The widespread use of covert surveillance and coercion in a society indicates that the forces that bind it together have become even less legitimate than those that link hostile belligerents in the traditional context of war.

Authority, however, is no less dangerous because it lacks legitimacy; rather, because of its own anxieties, it is more dangerous. The more sensitive and intelligent young people I know today consider themselves to be living in some degree the lives of outlaws. They attempt to resign themselves to the prospects of being busted for smoking pot or dropping acid, imprisoned for draft evasion either directly or under a loose charge of conspiracy, or locked away in a concentration camp if resistance to the Vietnam war or revolt in the urban slums results in the declaration of a State of National Emergency or invocation of the Internal Security Act of 1950. All these are valid fears. There *is* real danger of becoming a political prisoner in the United States today through the normal operation of due process. Our military adventures and our treatment of poor and black people are political questions, and therefore offenses related to opposition to such policies are political offenses. It is less clear that classifying marijuana as a "dangerous drug"—in the absence of substantial evidence to that effect— and making its use a felony, and its distribution under some circumstances punishable by life imprisonment, are legal definitions designed to curb political offenses. But they are, and the very fact that the political character of such laws seems paradoxical makes the political function of the pot issue worth scrutinizing.

Smoking marijuana is essentially a ritual action by which young people assert a moral position. Careful research has shown that both the dangers and joys associated with its use have been grossly exaggerated. The satisfactions it affords are derived far less from its mildly stimulating effect on the central nervous system— which may be agreeable or disagreeable, depending on the circumstances—than from the sense of affirming a particular view of the world and of one's place in it. Potblowing is ideological; examination of the ideology it expresses reveals several characteristic components. The most important of these are:

1) People who are enjoying themselves without harming others have an inalienable right to privacy.

2) A drug whose effect is to turn its users inward upon their own experience, enriching their fantasy life at the expense of their sense of the need to achieve or relate to others, is as moral as alcohol, which encourages a false gregariousness and increasingly pugnacious or competitive behavior.

3) Much of the solicitude of the older generation for the welfare of the young merely expresses a desire to dominate and control them for the sake of adult interests and the preservation of adult status and authority.

Pot is clearly less dangerous than pot-busts. It is also less dangerous to youth than the Selective Service System; parents who become hysterical and punitive about the dangers of drug abuse while being equally insistent that their sons go quietly to Vietnam when summoned are more concerned with the embarrassment of having children who are in trouble with the law than with their children's welfare. So we are back again to the issue of legitimacy, which is what the potblower's ideology basically questions. On their own terms, there can be no doubt that their position is valid: there are no demonstrable dangers to either the individual or society sufficient to justify or even explain the treatment accorded marijuana users. The effects of the drug are less obnoxious than those of alcohol; the solicitude of adults masks intense hostility and anxiety.

Institutionalized hostility toward marijuana users is intelligible, however, when the potblower's ideology is considered in relation to the class structure of American society. For that ideology expresses essentially an upper-middle to upper-class attitude toward life; indeed, for this century, it expresses one that is remarkably aristocratic. To value privacy and a rich inner life at the expense of achievement and the development of social skills in manipulating and competing with others—to value these is to reject the fundamental and official attitudes of American society, to fly in the face (and perhaps up the nose) of the school system, the Little League and the core virtues of the Land of Opportunity. The fact that marijuana is too mild a drug to do much for the fantasy-life does not affect the controversy. People get out of psychedelic drugs about what they expect and the use of marijuana has evolved in such a way that custom provides what the drug cannot—as it does for alcohol. Pot-parties have therefore become almost a photographic negative of cocktail parties: communal experiences at which the joint is passed from mouth to mouth like a peace pipe or communion cup; the scene is tranquil rather than gregarious, with no one-upping permitted; there is not even much moving around.

Pot, then, both evokes and symbolizes a whole set of attitudes and behavior that are anathema to the lower-middle classes: laziness and fantastic ease, grooving with one's neighbor instead of competing with him, drifting into bed with the partner of your choice rather than conning her into it as proof of your none-too-evident manhood. Pot-busts have become primarily a form of interclass hostility, in which the working class attacks the sloth, depravity and decadence of gilded, long-haired youth.

Interclass hostility of this kind is ancient, of course. What is novel, and very dangerous, in the form of pot-bust is that the customary class roles have been fundamentally reversed. For here it is the lower of the adversary classes which, armed with legitimacy, attacks the upper in the name of law and order. And the upper defends itself, when it does so at all, by appealing to such values as civil liberty, the right to privacy, and freedom from arbitrary search and seizure which, although recognized in general terms in the Constitution or reflected in certain court decisions, have never been accepted by the American masses which see them as essentially a form of privilege.

And so they are; and this is the heart of the conflict. For what American society most apparently lacks today is a device by which social class differences may be legitimated. This, in fact, is what our institutions have evolved, since Jackson's time, to prevent. Privilege in America is illegitimate *per se*. Or in de Tocqueville's words, written in Jackson's day:

> The Americans hold, that, in every state, the supreme power ought to emanate from the people; but when once that power is con-

stituted, they can conceive, as it were, no limits to it, and they are ready to admit that it has the right to do whatever it pleases. They have not the slightest notion of peculiar privileges granted to cities, families or persons: their minds appear never to have foreseen that it might be possible not to apply the same laws to every part of the state and to all its inhabitants.

This is not quite accurate. The Bill of Rights *does* conceive of limits to the supreme power of the people, and attempts to establish them—which is why the working class so often perceives the Supreme Court as opposed to law and order. The people certainly *do* have a notion of peculiar privileges granted to cities, families or persons—it is what they are most determined to prevent. They *do* foresee that it might be possible *not* to apply the same laws to every part of the state, and to all its inhabitants—which is why they enjoy lurid fantasies of the university as a privileged sanctuary for draft-dodgers, addicts and perverts. What they *don't* grant, even as a possibility, is that such privileges, and such a sanctuary, might have social value.

And for most of them, perhaps it would not. This is not an issue that need be debated, for American society is as receptive to the claim of vested interest as it is hostile to that of privilege. There are social classes in America as elsewhere, and a society that recognizes and defers to the special interests and needs of oil-producers, speculative builders and labor unions can hardly justify rejection of the special interests of middle-class youth, which sorely needs a place to call its own. American society as a whole would surely be far better off if its most sensitive and articulate youth did not feel themselves to be outlaws. No more need be demanded on behalf of hippies or turned-on youth than is accorded Standard Oil or the friendly Chase Manhattan

Bank: that their needs be recognized and reflected in the law of the land, and that they be allowed to go about their business unmolested without having to prove that what is good for them is good for the entire world.

But even this cannot be vouchsafed under our system. The answer adults give the beleaguered and fugitive young when finally forced to admit that the marijuana laws are Draconian and irrational, and the Selective Service Act capricious and inequitable, is to assert that for the sake of a stable and orderly society even unjust and unwise laws must be respected, and that procedures exist by which laws may be changed to make them wiser and more just. Unfortunately the idea that unwise and unjust laws—which reflect the hostilities and assuage the inferiority feelings and envy of the masses—can be effectively changed by due process and lawful means in a mass democracy is probably false. American law and public policy are almost always unresponsive to moral issues or minority needs, unless these find expression in terms of raw power. The fall of the Johnson administration, and subsequently of the Democratic party, under the impact of war protest may seem to belie this statement; so may the actual social progress the nation has made in the past fifty years. It is the blindness of the New Left to this record of past achievement, in fact, which most offends the surviving members of the Old Left. But neither case is a convincing indication that the American social or legal structure might be capable of a generous response to the demands of dissenting middle-class youth today. It seems very obvious that the Johnson administration would have been unaffected had the Vietnam war been prosecuted more successfully. Failure is punished by the electorate; but the war protest did not occasion the failure. Lyndon Johnson's defeat was not brought about by Benjamin Spock, Tom Hayden or Eugene McCarthy, but by the Vietnamese themselves. And they did not do it by winning their case before the bar of American public opinion or through the channels of American legal process.

The accomplishments of the Old Left are more solid, and unquestionably theirs. It is quite true that virtually all the social legislation they fought for in the thirties—against opposition fully as repressive as anything the New Left faces today—has not only been enacted but is now taken wholly for granted. What is sad, as Norman Thomas observed a few years before his death, is that nobody seems to have much pleasure out of it. But the goals of the New Left have a different political, and a different moral, significance than those of the Old; their tasks are not really comparable and they cannot really be allies.

Broadly speaking, the reforms of the thirties were economic and addressed to the improvement of social justice and the abatement of the grossest economic insecurity. What was achieved was solid, and new to a country which still provides much less in the way of social services, especially to the ill and aged, than an Englishman or Scandinavian would expect as a matter of right. In any case, the radicals of the thirties emphasized economic need and the improvement of the political power of the working class far more than civil rights, civil liberty or personal freedom. This was not because they were oblivious of these issues, but because they saw economic threat and vulnerability to poverty and economic pressure as the most serious threats to freedom. Job security and a decent wage, and essential social services, were to serve as shields against coercion

by bosses and the slings and arrows of outrageous
fortune. The Wagner Act and' the Federal
Minimum Wage Law were thought of not only as
guaranteeing certain important economic and political rights but also as part of the foundation on
which human liberty would rest.

As such, they have not been particularly effective. They serve as necessary instruments of
social justice in guaranteeing certain important
economic rights to the organized working class,
which is quite sufficient to justify them as legislation. But the working class has not proved to be
devoted to liberty; it is more inclined to be devoted to George Wallace or Mayor Daley. It
supports the war more zealously than the finan-
cial and industrial leadership of the country—a
paradox in terms of the stereotypes of the thirties,
which envisioned rough, honest, warmhearted
labor as the undauntable defender of peace and
international brotherhood against the rapacity of
capitalist warmongers. The capitalist warmongers
have proved rapacious enough. Nevertheless, I
do not think the American economy as a whole
is as committed to a policy of perpetual military
and political malevolence as the mass of the
American people; it is too easy to conceive of
other and more pleasant ways of profiting by our
not-altogether-free associations with our neigh-
bors. Where generals and corporate executives
support the Vietnam war out of economic and
status interests, both labor leaders and the working-class people one meets from day to day ac-
tively hate the draft-dodgers, peaceniks and
troublemakers who harass their country while
their boy is risking his life to defend it against the
savage and treacherous gook. *If he hadn't—if
he had ever started to talk like those long-haired
punks, they'd have had his ass themselves.* How-

ever the various factors add, support for the war is now strongest in the working class, at least among parents; their sons, chased by the draft, may be less enthusiastic. But resistance to the war remains primarily a middle-class value.

The reforms of the Old Left have thus added to the difficulties of the New by greatly strengthening the political power of what has proved to be the most repressive segment of the population —the real control-addicts, in William Burroughs' phrase: the supporters of law and order, so long as the law does not shackle their local police or protect fresh kids and hippies. The reforms of the Old Left have created also one final problem of legitimacy that the New Left is, I think, reluctant to face. For the Old Left reforms proved ultimately popular; they benefitted the masses at the expense of the classes, which not only gave the old radicals great satisfaction, it made their programs legitimate *per se*. They were on the side of democracy and they knew it; with the final triumph of FDR they could prove it. It is true that the forces of law were often arrayed against them, sometimes with a brutality equal—discounting the greater technological efficiency of the sixties—to anything the war-resisters encounter now. But when this happened in the thirties, just as when it happend later to civil-rights workers in the South, it was the law itself which had become illegitimate. This thought affords little protection to the body in confronting a group of murderous sheriff's deputies, but it does enhance the victim's self-esteem.

What seems to be the hardest today for young radicals to face, in their conviction that authority has become illegitimate, is the implication that the source of the illegitimacy is the American democratic process itself. It is one thing to assert that "the system" is corrupt, that the mass media conceal essential data and misrepresent what they do report, that political parties do not respond to the will of the electorate. It is another, and more difficult for a radical American, to grant that what is wrong with America may be characteristic of mass democracy itself.

Yet this seems to be the more valid conclusion. The mass media, for example, do not, I think, mislead people so much as they confirm them in the fantasies they wish to hold. When, as in the Chicago Convention coverage, they do not, all hell breaks loose as the public, in paroxysms of rage and self-pity, demands that its prejudices be confirmed. The public does not accept discordant interpretations of reality any more than a neurotic patient accepts an unwelcome interpretation; it was Walter Cronkite, not the public, who learned from the experience. And the American political process *does* respond to the will of the people; it is the mass of the people that does not respond to the moral imperatives of Vietnam and the plight of the poor and the black —or, rather, it responds with greater hostility as its own destructiveness mounts.

As the twentieth century, along perhaps with everything else, approaches its conclusion, it becomes apparent that democracy and fascism are not contrasting and opposing political systems, but different stages of evolution in the responsiveness of society to the fears, envies and resentments that pervade the lives of lower status groups. Democratic political structures are devised to legitimate the demands to which these feelings naturally give rise, and to increase the

political power of the masses, and hence their
capacity to command a better life. But in a society as open, invidious and competitive as ours,
the kinds of people who succeed are usually incapable of responding to human demands; and
the political power of the masses is used merely
to express the hatreds and the envy, and to
destroy anything that looks like genuine human
satisfaction, especially among the more vulner-
able members of the higher social classes. Higher
status youth—whose style of life infuriates the
working class and whose status by no means
compensates for their political helplessness as a

disfranchised group with few established civil
rights in law—have become the chief target of
the working-class sense of outrage and defeat.
It is difficult for white, middle-class parents to
imagine—and most don't want to—the degree of
harassment to which their adolescent children are
subjected by hostile and vigilant school authorities, and by police who feel, and are, perfectly
free to disperse groups of youngsters whose behavior is not at all threatening and who could
not, if adults, be held to have given probable
cause for suspicion of any offense.

Tyranny has taken many forms in history, but
the graceless vulgarity and egregious, clumsy
brutality of fascism are its most hideous form;
and these grow best out of the democratic process
itself. The masses came onto the stage of history
too late to be credited with having invented
tyranny—even the Russians have made no such
claim—but they have made something new and
more terrible of it by depriving it of style.

Those who complain of the failures of democracy are expected to provide a better political
plan and, even more confidently, expected to recoil in fear or perplexity from the demand that
they do so. Winston Churchill's much-quoted
comment that democracy is the worst system
of government in the world—except for all the
others—is supposed to have settled the matter.

But, in fact, there is no reason to feel em-
barrassed by this demand. Our political system,
like the rest of our society, has not become the
way it is in response to free and conscious choice,
and—unless we commit national suicide—it cannot be transformed by an act of will. It reflects,
rather, the effects of years of use and abuse, in-

sight and misunderstanding, discipline and indul-
gence—both often equally ill-considered—of its
inherited structures. There is no question of
choosing elitism or oligarchy or fascism or anything else instead of democracy. There is only
the question of how our present democratic system can respond to the demands placed on it by
the needs of the people whose lives it affects,
including those subject to its military and economic caprice who do not live within our borders.
It is not possible to change or exchange political
systems at will—even revolution does nothing
like this; the new one grows back, often mon-
strously deformed, on the roots of the old.

The comprehensive public school, in its commendable attempt to give children of all social
classes some experience of one another's lives,
has become an institution in which lower- and
upper-class children alike find themselves held
hostage—if they do not escape—to the values
and behavior patterns prized by the lower-middle
class and imposed by it as a universal norm of
conduct and moral judgment. Release with a
satisfactory credential depends on the student's
good conduct, and that of his parents, in not rejecting those norms or the values of the school
system itself.

The pattern of anxieties thus established in
the name of socialization has done much to
cement our society together—as well as to make
it more rigid when facing the need to devise
alternative norms. But that need is now pressing,
and the society is coming apart anyway. A major
force in its disruption is the irritation that the
upper and lower classes feel with each other; our
society is splitting right down the middle-middle.
And in a society that denies the legitimacy, if
not the very existence, of class interests, and

whose political leaders prattle of "law and order" as a remedy for "violence in the streets"—as if they had not seen a dozen times by now that the violence in the streets is often committed by the forces of law and order—nothing realistic can be done to recognize the serious nature of the conflict between those interests, or to resolve it.

It is almost certain that any effective measures to keep the American social system from bitter dissolution must indeed transcend present structural limits and political arrangements. The crucial question is whether this is possible. The present political structure of America is precisely what is wrong, and there is no *a priori* reason to assume that it bears within itself the seeds of its own reform. But I am sure that if any radical improvement in the quality of our national life can be made—and our survival depends on this—the devices by which it can be done will seem outrageous, and will, indeed, cause widespread outrage. But as perhaps most surviving American Indians and Vietnamese might agree, there is no great risk in devising a system more outrageous than that which America already has, and has had for nearly two centuries.

The Odds Against Women

By Ruth R. Hawkins

Of all the forms of discrimination in American life today, none remains more pervasive or more invidious than that directed against women. In industry, government and academia, women by and large are excluded from positions of power, as defined by salary, prestige and decision-making authority. There is as much sexual segregation in jobs now as sixty years ago, and although one-third of all women now work, most are still restricted to occupations defined as "feminine." In some instances women have been allowed to take over such previously "male" occupations as elevator operators, or have been recruited for such monotonous new jobs as key punch operators. Occupations that segregate heavily have been growing faster than those that do not. Dale Hiestand, in his study of employment opportunities for minorities (*Economic Growth and Employment Opportunities for Minorities,* New York, Columbia University Press, 1964), shows that in occupations in which incomes increase most rapidly, the acceptance of women is very slow. On the other hand, men enter jobs in which income rises rapidly whether or not they have been traditionally female occupations. Men, for example, now comprise the majority of secondary school teachers, and the nursing profession now wants to recruit men because only then will wages and hours improve.

Women now earn 40 percent of the bachelor degrees awarded, but their degrees aren't much help. Men right out of college are recruited for executive training, while women with the same qualifications are offered secretarial jobs. The American woman's share of the employment market has risen in recent years, but her share of professional and technical jobs has actually declined. Women are found predominantly in the less well-paid, uncompetitive jobs; they are more often overqualified in their work, and their median salary is below that of American men, both white and black. Sixty-six percent of employed women with from one to three years of college, 20 percent of employed women with a college degree, and 7 percent of employed women with one or more years beyond the first degree are sales ladies, office clerks, nursemaids and household cooks.

Despite professions to the contrary, the academic world is not exempt from such inequality. In 1966, two-thirds of the master's degrees and 88 percent of the doctorates were awarded to men. In 1965, of a total university enrollment of 2.3 million students, two-thirds of the places were held by men; at professional schools, 78 percent of the students were men.

These figures reflect academic quotas on women, higher standards of admission for women, denial of loans and fellowships, discouragement of part-time study, and course scheduling and other procedures geared to the service of men. The percentage of women graduate students shows only a slight improvement between 1956 (28 percent) and 1965 (30 percent), despite the unprecedented overall growth in that period. Alice Rossi, using data from a survey of forty thousand men and women of the class of 1961 three years after graduation, found that ambitious women who aspire to careers meet subtle and overt forms of punishment rather than encouragement and support. In her words, if a woman graduate student shows commitment and independence, faculty men call her an "unfeminine bitch," while woman graduate students who are quiet and unassertive are described by their male professors as "lacking ambition." Maria Goeppert Mayer, the only woman since Madame Curie to win the Nobel prize in physics, has said: "I sensed the resentment of the role of women in American academic life so I learned to be inconspicuous."

Graduate schools, indeed, are geared to the career development of men, who generally follow a relatively straightforward pattern with little consideration to their lives off the job, whereas the career and life patterns of women are complex and require greater flexibility on the part of academic institutions. Talcott Parsons and Gerald Platt's *The American Academic Profession: A Pilot Study* (Harvard Laboratory of Social Relations, 1968) appears to indicate that the intrinsic appeal of teaching to faculty members lies in the ways in which it perpetuates the system in which they are enthroned. Their mission is thus to make others into their own image, and students who do not fit the prevailing donnish mold are discouraged from pursuing academic careers.

It is not surprising, then, that women have a low percentage of faculty positions. Of the 494,514 places in 1964, men held 78 percent.

(The percentage reaches 90 percent in the most prestigious institutions.) It was not always so. In 1939, women held 30 percent of the faculty jobs—40 percent in 1879. In the early 1960's, however, 37 percent of the teaching and professional staff positions in colleges and universities were part-time, and women were—and are— heavily represented. In this group, of course, they are the expendables; those who are added or dropped in response to changes in enrollment or budgetary support. In addition, Jessie Bernard's study of academic women (*Academic Women,* The Pennsylvania State University Press, 1964) found that the faculty rank of women is inferior to that of men in all kinds of institutions, despite comparable qualifications and productivity. The median salary of women is one thousand dollars less than that of men. One factor, undoubtedly, is that when men fill a vacancy, they tend to seek people like themselves and do not consider untypical members of the guild, including women. The result is that women, although representing over 51 percent of the nation's population, are virtually shut out of the academic work force.

There are predictions, moreover, that in the 1970's the number of college teaching posts will be lower than the number of PH.D.'s available. In this case, the gap between men and women faculty members will widen, since women have gained scarcely 20 percent of the available places during the greatest expansion of higher education in this country. Further, in the 1970's the number of women seeking employment will be unprecedented. Not only will there be a continuation of the pattern of married women joining the work force as their children reach high school, but with the present decline in the birth rate and longer intervals between marriage and child bearing, there will be increasing numbers of young, childless married women, as well as young unmarrieds, seeking jobs.

In the face of these discouraging economic facts of life, the rise of militant feminist organizations such as The National Organization for Women (career women) and The Women's Liberation Front (undergraduate and graduate women students) is inevitable. Indeed, one could only conclude that American women would be suffering from the most debilitating masochism if they did not begin to organize to end this pervasive discrimination. On many campuses young feminists, learning from the techniques of black militants, are pressing for changes in admissions policy, for courses on women such as that initiated at the University of California at Los Angeles, and for hiring and promotion policies which will ensure that women have better representation in higher education. For example, a group in Buffalo has recommended that the State University of New York establish a college with a balanced faculty of men and women, a campus day-care center and a program of study on women.

The parallel between the treatment of blacks and women by our society was drawn by Gunnar Myrdal in an appendix to his classic, *The American Dilemma*. But it was put more dramatically by Eldridge Cleaver, who views the white man as establishing himself as the Omnipotent Administrator. The black man, sent to work in the fields, became the Supermasculine Menial, while the black woman, wearing Aunt Jemima's bandanna, was deposited in the kitchen, a self-reliant amazon. The white woman, ideally the beautiful

dumb blonde, was placed on a pedestal, weak-
minded and weak-bodied. "That is why when
you get down to the rest of it, the white man
does not want the black man, the black woman
or the white woman to have a higher education.
Their enlightenment would pose a threat to his
omnipotence," Cleaver says.

Feminists are concerned with what happens
to the relatively few women who do teach in colleges and universities. (Only 9 percent of the
full professors are women.) What are the existing
criteria for tenure, they ask, and what should
they be? Jessie Bernard's study found that academic women preferred to be teachers and were
more concerned with students, while men were
less responsive to students than to their professional peers. In the Parsons-Platt study, faculty
preferred to give more time to graduate than to
undergraduate students, and they indicated that
they would ideally invest more time in research
and scholarship than in teaching at any level.
Academic women publish proportionately less
than their male colleagues, and feminist organizations question the necessity of contributing to
the publication explosion as opposed to the
knowledge explosion to win promotion. For a
price is paid by faculty members who follow the
conventional focus on publications, honorary
awards and committee participation; the price
is a lopsided life of all work and little play or
family and community life.

> "Isn't it time the university [Alice Rossi has said],
> as the most farseeing of our social institutions, pre-
> pared itself for life in the post-industrial world . . .
> a compassionate world with the time, the room
> and the flexibility to create a style of living that
> permits men and women to live deeply and mean-
> ingfully at play and at home as well as at work?"

Aside from publication, what objective criteria exist for evaluating a professor for promo-

tion? None, really. It becomes, then, a question of how compatible are the views of the candidate, his life-style and personal relations with those of the tenured members of his department. In this subjective area, women are disadvantaged. There is often an inability on the part of the judges to distinguish between these women and their home-maker wives. And often the refusal to increase the salary of married academic women is not determined by performance, but by personal resentment of the higher style of life enjoyed by households containing two career people.

The goal of the new feminists is an ideological one: equality between the sexes. They are not interested in tinkering with short-run improvements in the status of women. For practical purposes, a certain amount of energy must be devoted to applying pressure on government and other institutions to undertake specific actions or to cease certain practices. But the long-range objective is to change society. The foundations of role differentiation between the sexes are increasingly challenged by medical and psychological research. If the present arrangements are not justified in psychology or physiology, then is it that our economy forces men to work at persistent levels of efficiency and creativity so that the present family system conveniently supports the occupational system?

College enrollment is expected to jump from 5.9 million in 1966 to 9.4 million in 1976, and this does not include efforts to enroll more students from disadvantaged backgrounds. There would thus seem to be a need to develop criteria for effective teaching of different kinds of students: the disadvantaged, the job-oriented, the gifted and the creative. And the question of men and women faculty members, with their special talents and instincts, is involved. But the agendas of faculty meetings rarely include such issues.

Just as blacks have resisted racial integration when it means becoming white to be accepted, the feminists are not seeking assimilation. They are pressing for a reexamination of the socialization process. No assumptions and no institutions are sacrosanct—not family, church, education or government. Feminism, in its broadest sense, is part of the ground swell for qualitative change in American society.

Are Academic Standards Obsolete?

By Nathan Glazer

Until quite recently, no one seriously questioned the traditional doctrine that academic ability should be the sole basis for gaining the payoffs and rewards of academic success. To have assumed otherwise could quite easily have subverted the whole academic enterprise. But the questioning of this most fundamental of educational concepts has become so powerful of late that we must now ask the inevitable question: If measuring people by academic performance no longer serves the wider goals of society, what then is to take its place? The choices, and the consequences, are among the most fundamental that face American higher education.

The traditional rules of the game are easily enough laid out. Educational institutions now grade students on the basis of their achievement. Grading constitutes the basis of their eligibility for admission to other academic institutions and special programs. Not only do the rewards of the educational system provide an opportunity for further education: admission to colleges, graduate schools, and professional schools is also generally held essential for securing a good job.

Grades by themselves do not seem to play a crucial role in determining one's future, except insofar as they are necessary for graduation from a university or college, or for judging one's eligibility for further education. Once one is admitted to a certain college, or graduate school, or professional school, and graduated from it, the grades received are soon forgotten. In England, the achievement of a first at Oxford or Cambridge is part of one's biography, and affects one's future. I suspect that graduation even as a summa cum laude from an American institution of high prestige plays little role in one's future career. For most people, the critical issue is getting in and getting out.

Until a few years ago, it was assumed almost without question that the aims of educational institutions should be to distribute their rewards on the grounds of educational ability alone, on academic ability, or more generally merit, as exhibited in school work and examinations. The common liberal—and educator's—view of the matter was that this desirable approach to the distribution of academic rewards stood in conflict with more conservative, reactionary, or even feudal practices which did not reward according to ability. If we look at some of the sociological literature on education of some years ago, we find that high school children of the better-off and better-connected and of the right ethnic background would get better grades, even though they didn't deserve them. Children of the poorer and more poorly connected and of the wrong ethnic background, on the other hand, would get worse grades, often equally undeserved.

Justice and efficiency seemed to have conjoined in demanding that academic ability be placed at the very top as the democratizing criterion for the distribution of rewards—grades, admissions, and diplomas. Justice demanded that these be given out on the basis of ability and effort, and not on the basis of class, background, or personal connection; and efficiency seemed to demand that the most able be rewarded so that they would find the place in society in which they could make their maximum contribution.

only because of a convention that distributes rewards unequally on the basis of academic abilities. Those holding this position might make this wager: "Distribute Harvard diplomas at random to every thousand graduates." Since they would then be treated as Harvard men, they would presumably achieve the same position Harvard men do under the present system. And, this argument would go, the world would be no better or worse off as a result. From this point of view, the Harvard diploma is a "certification" rather than an index to valuable and rare talents. Thus, we find a spreading notion among more radical critics that academic ability—whether or not it is culturally biased, whether or not it is influenced by teachers' expectations, whether or not it is uniquely valuable—is irrelevant to most important social functions. Diplomas might as well be distributed at random. The world would be no worse off. Indeed it might be better off, since those benefitting from a better position in life would then be selected at random, hence more justly, rather than on the basis of criteria linked to class, wealth, and race.

Fifth, we find an even more radical position which asserts not that the academic ability, as measured and rewarded, is irrelevant to the better performance of a contemporary society, but that it is all too relevant: it common argument made for higher education.

Reformers often argued that grading at the college level could not be completely fair, and that it led to the making of invidious distinctions. Thus, Bennington College used extended written evaluations instead of grades, a practice already common in progressive schools at the elementary and secondary level. But for purposes of providing a more widely acceptable academic coin, progressive schools generally prepared, along with the verbal evaluation, another simpler evaluation: a grade. Now we face far more powerful attacks, attacks which are well on the way to dissolving the powerful hold that academic ability has thrust on American educational institutions as a basis for academic success. These attacks are part of a massive new effort to right serious social wrongs.

E ducational institutions have not in the past offered much reward to blacks. They have not admitted them in proportion to their percentage in the population, rewarded them with grades distributed in the same way as the grades of white students, nor graduated them in comparable numbers. And the same can be said for Mexican-Americans, Puerto Rican-Americans, and American Indians. Racial discrimination by educational authorities and faculties has played a large but indeterminate role in giving such a poor return to black and other minority students.

But this past evidence of academic discrimination has been clearly overshadowed by a powerful body of evidence of the poor academic achievement of minority students. As we know, there is some interrelation between discrimination by educational authorities and poor academic achievement. Prejudice and discrimination sensed or felt may lead to poorer efforts and may inhibit achievement. But clearly, the tested results of academic ability play a substantial role in justifying differential rewards by educational institutions. To provide a better distribution of rewards by race requires a fundamental attack on the whole academic assumption of reward by ability.

Obviously, to many of us who have achieved some position by means of demonstrations of intellectual ability, and who have taken it for granted that ability is, or should be, the sole fair basis for the distribution of rewards, the new assumptions pose a disturbing development. Lines of battle are formed on almost every college campus, and at the lower education levels as well.

In the past, the practices that substituted class and ethnic criteria for academic ability were criticized because they served to keep down the poor and the ethnic.

Indeed, it was the American Jews, suffering most from such practices, who launched the most powerful attack on the use of any criteria but tested academic ability as a basis for academic rewards. In large measure they succeeded. Wherever tested academic ability and related talents play a role (tests for the civil service and the like), Jews and some other previously deprived ethnic groups—for example, Japanese-Americans—will do quite well.

But today, we see an interesting reversal: Now the emphasis on tested academic ability keeps out the *new* minority groups of America. Thus the attack on merit, which was largely a monopoly of the Right in the past, is today deployed by the Left. Now, the old arguments are supplemented by many new ones. It is now widely thought that we damage not only the less competent, the worse trained, those who for whatever reasons refuse to enter wholeheartedly into academic competition. We also damage, socially, the Negro, the Mexican-American, the Puerto Rican, the American Indian.

In one respect, there exists a parallel between the old underground arguments that were used to justify non-academic criteria for academic reward and those put forth today. Those who once asserted that class, religious and racial criteria should play a role in academic reward argued that this was necessary to maintain a given social structure. Thus it would have been quite outlandish if a disproportionate percentage of places in elite schools went to Jews. This would have led, it was said, to a split between the elite of property and power and the educated elite, producing conflict and subversion of the social structure. (In some measure, this is just what has happened.)

Today we are told, with some justice, that a narrow-minded insistence on academic criteria, at a time when the interests of the country demand a rapid rise by

minority groups to elite positions, will make it difficult
to develop a representative elite which will contribute to
the social stability of the country. To insist therefore on
academic criteria is once again to encourage instability.
In both cases, the old and the new arguments opt for a
greater disregard of academic ability in favor of social
stability, and that process which will best enhance it.

More incisive, perhaps, is the feeling of many people
that there exist no true or good tests for academic
ability. They make several assumptions. First, they argue, I.Q. and achievement tests are culturally biased. The
removal of these biases seems enormously difficult. Present tests are tests of exposure to a culture rather than a
pure reflection of innate ability. Under different cultural
circumstances, persons who score badly on present tests
might well emerge with great academic ability.

Second, it is said, tests and demonstrations of academic ability are influenced by the expectations of
teachers—expectations molded in a racist culture. These
expectations influence the child.

Third, academic ability itself, it is pointed out, is
only one of the capacities an educational system should
seek out, develop, judge and reward. Why should it be
given primacy? It is only one of a number of abilities
that should be valued by a society. Those who have been
impressed by the thesis of the cultural bias of tests have
tried to identify other talents that would be distributed
differently from academic ability through a population.
One, quite clearly, is athletic ability. Another is aesthetic
ability. A third, Christopher Jencks and David Riesman
point out, is the kind of interpersonal talent useful for
those who administer or lead organizations and who
must bring together the varied talents of many people.
Thus, a primacy on academic ability for the distribution
of educational rewards penalizes those with other valued
talents and prevents them from gaining a position suited
to their talents.

Fourth, a more sophisticated argument asserts that

tested academic ability is conceivably not related to *any* socially useful talents. If those who test high on academic ability achieve high positions, it may not be because of intrinsic merits that society needs and rewards, but only because of a convention that distributes rewards unequally on the basis of academic abilities. Those holding this position might make this wager: "Distribute Harvard diplomas at random to every thousand graduates." Since they would then be treated as Harvard men, they would presumably achieve the same position Harvard men do under the present system. And, this argument would go, the world would be no better or worse off as a result. From this point of view, the Harvard diploma is a "certification" rather than an index to valuable and rare talents. Thus, we find a spreading notion among more radical critics that academic ability—whether or not it is culturally biased, whether or not it is influenced by teachers' expectations, whether or not it is uniquely valuable—is irrelevant to most important social functions. Diplomas might as well be distributed at random. The world would be no worse off. Indeed it might be better off, since those benefitting from a better position in life would then be selected at random, hence more justly, rather than on the basis of criteria linked to class, wealth, and race.

Fifth, we find an even more radical position which asserts not that the academic ability, as measured and rewarded, is irrelevant to the better performance of a contemporary society, but that it is all too relevant: it enables corrupt and evil institutions in a corrupt and evil society to function better. In this view academic ability, whether a useful test or not, helps society select people for its wars, for profit-seeking, for environmental abuse, for those institutions which degrade human beings. Academic ability serves as a mechanism whereby those who can best serve in these varied capacities are rated and selected. In particular, those most suited to certain levels in a hierarchical society can be selected for their positions—those to be manipulated, those to serve the manipulators, those who manipulate directly—by means of an educational system that presumably operates on the basis of tested academic ability, but which actually, in a variety of ways—of which this may be one—rates people for a bad society.

In the present system, this radical thesis goes, it would be a real virtue to resist the sorting mechanisms that remove the rebellious as dropouts, that select the pliable for high school graduation, the somewhat more gifted for college and minor leadership positions, the most gifted for positions as the necessary mandarins and apologists for an evil society. While this is not a widely held position, the animus of radicals against the role of academic ability in education comes from just such reasoning.

I have recently had the opportunity to listen to the ideas of Ivan Illich, ideas which have a good deal in common with those of Paul Goodman and Edgar Friedenberg, but which go beyond the attack on selectivity to attack the whole system of schooling now fastened on the world—capitalist, communist, or third—as a means of legitimating and justifying a system of privilege, even in the minds of those who do not share in it. Illich argues against a graded curriculum which degrades all those who do not complete it (almost the entire population in developing countries); against an age-specific curriculum which dictates what should be learned at given ages; against compulsory attendance rules. He points out that this entire system is unjust and enormously expensive in terms of what it produces (literacy can be achieved at a fraction of the cost with which it is attained in school). One way of breaking the hold of schooling, he proposes, would be to ban discrimination based on schooling. He would agree that certain tasks need certain skills, but he would insist that each task be judged by its own tests, one of which might simply be observation on the job. He would want to see compulsory schooling abolished and education conducted in a variety of settings, particularly in work settings, as it was to a large extent in the past.

In Ivan Illich's educational millenium, the issue of rewards for tested academic ability would in large measure disappear. Academic ability would not be tested at all, except for jobs where it was directly relevant (academic jobs). It would become less valuable as less was offered for it. Schooling would be offered and taken voluntarily. But would the abolition of the monopolistic and expensive system of schooling lead to a larger reward for the now underrepresented minority groups? Is there not a relationship between the capacity to score high on tests of academic ability and the capacity to score high on most other kinds of tests? Are not some of the elements in tests of academic ability—the ability to read, to comprehend what one has read, to express oneself in writing, to follow directions—important abilities for many kinds of occupations? I am much more impressed with Illich's proposal to abolish the present system of schooling than with the possibility that this would significantly reduce the problems of differential rewards to groups in a multi-racial society.

After all this, what can be said for reward on the basis of academic ability? Clearly a good deal depends on one's sense of the complexity of the world. If one believes that the world is in a perilous situation, that there are problems which require great abilities of various kinds, one will probably look more favorably on the preservation of the process of selection. If, on the other hand, one believes that the world is fundamentally simple, that there are solutions available to our problems, then one will feel that the concern for selection is less important. In this view, equality would take a more dominant role, overcoming the unnecessary concern for efficiency or originality.

We have already suggested the first and perhaps the most important: the world has need for rare talents and abilities. By definition, these are not to be found in every man. They must be sought out, encouraged and developed, otherwise they would surface in insufficient quantity and quality. Tests of academic ability are adequate, if inexact, indexes to their presence, and the tests can probably be improved.

This is the classic and to my mind the basic argument for rewards on the basis of tested academic abilities. But there are others associated with some concentration of the academically able. Concentration provides an atmosphere which leads to greater accomplishments and higher peaks of developed talent. When artists are gathered together in art schools, the mere environment created by concentration presumably encourages each to do better. Similarly, when athletes of high ability are brought together, they do better than when they work in the company of athletes of mediocre ability. Finally, talented teachers are rare. The concentration of students of high ability, aided by a concentration of teaching talents, may encourage yet higher development.

Aside from the needs of the society, there remains the question of justice to the individual. Those who have displayed academic ability have often worked hard, foregone other gratifications, concentrated their efforts for certain goals. Is it right that they be treated the same way as those who have not? Admittedly, their achievement is based in part on native talent and early childhood exposure. But almost any student who enters a selective college or a selective graduate or professional school feels that his own effort has contributed in some degree to his fine achievements. What would be his reaction if he were told that that his own efforts and his own record of tested academic ability could play no role, or at the most a very reduced role, in his chances for educational rewards, and the other rewards associated with them?

Christopher Jencks points out that if we are interested in rewarding effort, we should do so directly, rather than by rewarding achievement, which is after all affected by inheritance, social background, and the like. Thus a system of reward by tested academic achievement is not the most efficient system of rewarding effort, even granted that effort does play some role.

Academic ability is also important as a basis for bringing together students who share that trait in common for the purpose of creating a feeling of community. Community-building in the modern world becomes more difficult as new considerations come into play to challenge older bases of association. Does the lottery system

of college admissions have much chance of helping create a sense of community? We have already challenged religious and racial bases of selection. Regional bases of selection, while common, are also eschewed by many institutions. Now selection on the basis of academic criteria is attacked. As we reduce the characteristics which members of a student body hold in common—a desirable trend in general, because education arises from a wider range of experience—should we set a limit to this expansion of types of students admitted? Opportunities for education are reduced when all students are selected from a narrow, common background. Opportunities for education, however, may be overwhelmed when the varieties of backgrounds and interests and cultures are so diverse that very little basis for community-making exists.

Finally, there is a question of faculty morale. Certainly faculty morale is based in part on the knowledge that there has been some basis for the selection of students. Many faculties at institutions of all levels seem to find some support for morale when considering the nature of their student bodies. But morale is based on features other than the academic ability of the students, and these other elements will be brought into play when academic ability is known to be low.

Do the same mechanisms operate among students? Here again things look different from the level of Harvard than from that of San Jose State or Los Angeles City College. From the level of the highly selective institution, the inferior institution seems a purgatory for the students. For the students themselves, it is an opportunity. There are people and institutions above, and people and institutions below. I am not sure any measure of student morale at institutions of different levels of selectivity would show a clear relationship between morale and selectivity. Perhaps the key element is whether the student sees himself in a relatively open system. The actual pattern in a system of graded academic institutions, such as the public institutions in California, is for students to enter where they can, and work themselves up the system, if they can.

The fact that morale is maintained in institutions of low selectivity suggests to me that to eliminate selectivity would *reduce* the morale of faculty and students presently in institutions of high selectivity without necessarily doing much to *raise* it in institutions with low admission standards. In other words, hierarchy itself, in the form of institutions of different degrees of selectivity, when combined with a system that permits easy transfer from one to the other—as in the state of California—seems to do more, to my mind, to maintain morale throughout the system than would graded institutions without transfer (as in Europe), or institutions all of the same rank, in which one mechanism to motivate students and the faculty teaching them would have disappeared.

John H. Gagnon, following up on research of James Davis, gives a rather ingenious argument for a hierarchy of institutions of different degrees of selectivity (see "The Uses of Failure," *Change*, May-June 1969). The argument is that this serves to provide abler people for occupations of poorer reputation (for example, teaching, social work) than they would otherwise get. Davis and Gagnon point out that, whatever the level of selectivity of institutions, all grade on a curve. Thus, the experience of "success" and "failure" tends to be roughly equally distributed within institutions. Even though only valedictorians get into Harvard, many will discover they are not as good as the best, and even though only persons in the bottom half of their graduating high school classes get into other institutions, some will find they are doing quite well. One adaptation to failure in highly selective institutions is abandonment of the "hard" fields (e.g., physics) to go into the "soft" fields (e.g., sociology). Thus the presumably able students who have gained

admission to highly selective institutions enter occupations they would not have entered if they had been in
institutions where they were among the best. Similarly,
better students in less selective institutions are marked
out because of the surrounding mediocrity, and tend to
do better going into occupations of higher prestige than
they would have had they been selected for high-prestige
institutions.

One defense against reduced standards (given particular prominence by a speech of Vice President Agnew) is
that reduced standards for admission to institutions may
mean reduced standards for graduation. The actual practices of colleges with high standards suggest that this is
not likely to happen. In general, institutions with high
standards of selection have developed practices and traditions which make it very difficult for them to drop
students for inadequacy. Once admitted into the most
selective undergraduate, graduate and professional programs, there is almost a guarantee that one will graduate.
Generally only refusal to continue work at all, rather
than work at a low level, leads to expulsion.

Would these practices and expectations change
when students of lesser ability were introduced? It
would be difficult to change them, for political, social
and humane reasons. In some public universities with
open enrollment, one-third or more of the students are
failed in their first year. This is not a simple process. Not
all teachers have the nerve to fail students without
mercy, simply to reduce numbers and thus do in the first
year what has not been done by the admissions process.

Some of the debate over open admissions has not
faced up to the costs of this process, and to its requirements for teachers of a temperament that may not be
common. On a recent visit to one institution, I was
impressed that two teachers seemed to have taken upon
themselves a substantial part of this task, by maintaining
in their own classes high standards which substantial
numbers of the new freshmen could not meet. I suspect

there are some deeper costs to such an approach—for teachers and students as well as institutions.

I myself am convinced that it would be a sadder and grayer world if there were no reward for abilities. Certain prizes are so august that most of us are delighted to see them conferred and feel no sense of envy when they are given. This is the case with Nobel prizes. Those scientists who are passed over, we now know, may often feel a sense of injustice, of having been beaten out by shady politics or unfair publicity tactics. Yet would we give up the opportunity to give rewards, with all that means for the encouragement of effort and high standards, so as to eliminate the feelings of injustice and envy that inevitably arise when we single out some for rewards? We could fully eliminate such responses only if we refused to single out anyone, except by chance, or if we distributed rewards that were meaningless, that had lost all value. Undoubtedly, we see in contemporary society a withdrawal from the acceptance of common standards, a weakening of our sense of rightness or justice in making distinctions. But is this not often owing to our own cowardice which makes it difficult for us to face those to whom we have not given high prizes, as well as to our inner doubts as to the proper standards to apply?

It is questionable whether those in minority groups who now attack standards as being unfair and unjust would want to eliminate them entirely. Like men everywhere, they also seek distinctions and rewards. Are they ready to accept a life situation where all rewards become meaningless because they are distributed at random?

Some compromise solution to this dilemma is possible, of course. A larger role can be given to factors aside from tested academic ability. Thus, students can be admitted to institutions on the basis of abilities that some teachers or counsellors have detected that do not as yet (and may never) express themselves in formal work. (At the University of California, which operated a system of admissions on the basis of merit alone, 2 percent of students were admitted on the basis of criteria outside the formal system. A few years ago this was raised to 4 percent. There are strong demands that it go still higher. In the 2 percent period, it was generally believed that the special admission privilege was used to permit athletes to get in. More recently, it has been used to allow larger numbers from deprived minority groups to enter.)

Other institutions use other mechanisms, but everywhere the system of admissions by tested academic ability is being supplemented by new bases for admission. In effect, educational rewards, if we use admission as one index, are now granted to a considerably lesser degree than a few years ago on the basis of tested academic ability. The main problem arises when we begin to use the new bases for admission for larger proportions of students. When 20, or 30 or 50 percent of students are admitted outside the system of tested academic ability, then I would guess that some of the negative processes will begin to operate—the impact on teachers' morale, the effect on the culture and temperament of the student group, and the exclusion of others of higher tested academic ability.

Our dilemma has become so acute because we have allowed institutions of higher education to play a larger role in determining men's fate than they ought to. At one time those children who were expected to be something of a failure were sent to institutions of higher education, to be prepared for the ministry or for occupations as teachers of Greek and Latin. Able men went into politics, the army, the family business. There were other routes upward, and because there were, the colleges were left to apply their own standards in peace, irrelevant as they might have been, because the rewards they distributed did not mean that much. This was at a time when only a small fraction of the population, and generally only children of the rich and well-born, went on to higher education, and the role of higher education in society itself was radically smaller than it is today.

Perhaps it is primarily because the colleges and universities have taken over so critical a role in the careers of tens of millions of people that their ability to maintain the primacy of tested academic achievement as a means of distributing rewards is disintegrating. I believe that if colleges and universities remain, as they have become, the major means by which a rough status is distributed among men, they cannot maintain the primacy of tested academic ability, except in those areas where they have a strong case that tested academic talents and skills are necessary for further advancement—particularly in the sciences. Otherwise, why, in a time of social revolution, would and should they be allowed to apply *their* standards for selection? These are standards which may be suited for further school work, but are only doubtfully suited for determining the distribution of status and power in society. There is now a powerful drive to have blacks play a larger role in society. It is inconceivable that academic standards, which for various reasons select only a small number, will be allowed to stand in the way.

One can foresee developments along a number of lines: tested academic ability will play a smaller role in selection to institutions of higher education. Employers who have leaned heavily on the system of higher education as a sieve for selection will have to develop their own standards (and in doing this they too will be challenged by the attack on testing). Attending a post-high school institution with some educational objectives will become nearly universal, and, as it becomes universal, experiences that we hardly considered education some years ago will become more prominent (political activity, emotional training, amusements and leisure). It will also be increasingly difficult for any institution to insist on academic ability alone as means for admission or, for that matter, graduation; all institutions will become more representative of the national mix.

Institutions that insist on maintaining high standards may only be allowed to do so if they, in effect, take a vow that the privileges they grant—for admission, study, signs of qualification—will not be allowed to determine men's fates. In this sense, they will become more like the monasteries of the Middle Ages, in which poverty and humility were linked with the free opportunity to edit and study old manuscripts.

We return to our original question: Is the world hard or easy? Can we maintain a society of some degree of peace, material comfort, humanity, without a means for rewarding it, without a ladder for those who have done best? Or is nature so bountiful, our present achievements in technology so adequate—and so simple, human nature so benign—that we can conclude that our system of education is meaningless for any decent human ends, its harshness simply a reflection of selfishness and malignity, and that we lose nothing and gain a great deal by abandoning its selective features? We are about to find out, and much of the future of American higher education hangs on the outcome.

The Community College In Search of Identity

by Arthur M. Cohen and Florence B. Brawer

Although community colleges have existed since the turn of the century, until recently they reposed in the backwaters of American social thought, away from the main currents of higher education. The general histories of the subject allowed them hardly more than a footnote. The few books written about them were hortative, not analytical. For decades these colleges went their own way, unexamined and practically ignored by the broader education community.

However, the situation now has shifted markedly. The two-year colleges have not only become visible but are being embraced by people who earlier had been hardly more than aware that they existed. And they are being called upon—and are responding to the call—to perform many functions for which they were not originally conceived. The question now is whether they can live up to all the expectations that people have of them—and more importantly, whether they should try.

Consider what has happened to community colleges recently on the federal scene alone: when the Elementary and Secondary and Higher Education Acts were passed in 1965, the community colleges were scarcely mentioned. They simply fell between the planks of the high schools on the one side and the liberal arts colleges and universities on the other. But within the past two years, President Nixon called for new legislation to support the colleges, the first

Comprehensive Community College Act was introduced in Congress and a Director of Community College Education was appointed in the U.S. Office of Education.

One reason the community colleges have drawn this attention is that they provide a way of rebutting increasing demands for open college admissions. Despite all the furor of recent years, for example, entrance to the University of California is as restrictive as ever. But the university can afford to be exclusive because California has ninety-three junior colleges in which anyone who has graduated from high school and/or attained age 18 may enroll. On the other hand, the doors to the City University of New York have been blown wide open. New York had fewer community colleges, and these had selective admissions policies so demands for open enrollment in the university were therefore both more clamorous and more difficult to deny.

In other states, too, demands for open admissions have stimulated university administrators and trustees to look about for places to shunt applicants. Their eyes inevitably fall on the community colleges. Where state master plans for higher education have been developed, respective functions are specified for two-year, four-year and graduate institutions. The two-year institutions are to enable the majority of post secondary students to continue their the one side and the liberal arts colleges and universities on the other. But within the past two years, President Nixon called for new legislation to support the colleges, the first Comprehensive Community College Act was introduced in Congress and a Director of Community College Education was appointed in the U.S. Office of Education.

One reason the community colleges have drawn this attention is that they provide a way of rebutting increasing demands for open college admissions. Despite all the furor of recent years, for example, entrance to the University of California is as restrictive as ever. But the university can afford to be exclusive because California has ninety-three junior colleges in which anyone who has graduated from high school and/or attained age 18 may enroll. On the other children, regardless of academic aptitude or previous school achievement, will have a convenient and accredited institution next door. And since few community college students or faculty members have organized marches protesting social inequities, legislators can safely support their development without facing charges of coddling dissidents.

Leaders of industry view the colleges as institutions to provide workers trained at public expense. Elected officials as well are on record as saying that much greater emphasis ought to be placed on technical training in the community colleges. Substantial funds for vocational programs are available through state and federal programs and college leaders are not remiss in applying for them. Accordingly, many institutions have more than one hundred separate vocational training sequences, and new programs are organized every time a need appears for different skills.

The community college holds promise for graduate students, too. The current job market at the universities and liberal arts colleges is tight. But community colleges continue to expand and to employ increasing numbers of new faculty.

To the young, the community college also promises second and third chances. A student may fritter away his or her time in high school, make a poor academic record and drop off the formal educational track. But whenever the student is ready to come back, there is a community college that will admit him. This standing prospect of absolution for past academic sins has also had a marked influence on the high school student, who can no longer be admonished that he or she might not be able to "get into college" without a satisfactory record. The decision to commit oneself toward or away from further schooling can thus be postponed almost indefinitely.

The community college, then, has something for everyone. It offers the university a safety valve, the employer a trained worker, the graduate-degree holder a job. It offers a place for the taxpayer's children, and second, third, infinite chances to people who, for whatever reason, want to go back to school. For the community at large, it promises academic and cultural upgrading. Even the police like it because young people, off the streets and under institutional custody, are less likely to get into trouble. Small wonder the community college has become everybody's darling.

But one should be wary of the tendency to look at a single institution as both a way of coping with frustration and a repository of hope. Enthusiasm can be a mask concealing the intention to unload the undesirable.

Shouldn't one be wildly enthusiastic about another institution that promises to relieve one of an onerous responsibility? The university has never done an adequate job of educating the student of marginal academic ability. Few people within it have wanted to assume such a challenge. But where it has relinquished this task to the community college, it has been able to cover its own failings.

The enthusiastic giving of tasks—and the equally enthusiastic acceptance of them—has already proved debilitating to the community college. It has led to ambiguity of intent because many of the tasks are contradictory. How can one institution simultaneously select, train, maintain custody and enhance development of the same group of people? The junior colleges are in a trap—partly of their own making, partly because university, community, state and national leaders have been only too willing to assign the most difficult educational tasks to them. They are being killed with kindness and the more responsibilities assigned to them, the less likely they are to meet any of them successfully.

Most of the eight hundred community colleges do try. Forced to take the brunt of expanding enrollments in higher education, they cast about for new procedures to handle the crowds of people who seek job training, experiences relevant to their fancy or simply a place to be while awaiting marriage, a job, the Army or admission to a university. In their effort to service their students, they adopt various curricular and instructional techniques and frequently invent their own. If anything is happening in instruction anywhere, some community college is likely to be doing it. Community colleges are the foremost enthusiasts of instructional systems, auto-instructional programming, mechanized laboratories and every possible type of machine that can be adapted for instructional use. Behavioral objectives—anathema to most university professors—are widely used. Some community college districts even budget for innovation and offer instructors extra pay for developing new types of presentations. Short courses, non-punitive grading, sensitivity training, remedial, sub-remedial, and sub-sub-remedial sequences—few programmatic schemes are too daring for these colleges to try.

Despite all efforts, however, the colleges have difficulty in demonstrating their success. They are widely accessible, but their student dropout figures are astronomical. They create new programs readily, but no one collects data on the extent of student learning. Their vocational programs are well developed, but there are few takers, the main path to skilled employment still being through apprenticeships and on-the-job training. And their guidance activities, ostensibly designed to enhance students' self-understanding, do little more than sort students into the various programs the colleges offer. The opportunity to enroll is given; the responsibility for the outcomes is not assumed. Whatever achievement there is seems to lie primarily in their good intent.

It is easy to see why the community college cannot possibly succeed in fulfilling everyone's expectations. Why then does it readily take on all the hard tasks that other social agencies refuse to deal with? A partial answer can be found in the colleges' need for acceptance. For years community college faculty and administrators sought the status that went with being part of higher education. But for years they were rebuffed—unable to dispel their "high school with ashtrays" image.

In their striving for full partnership, they became overly eager to assume a little of almost everything—like the newcomer who wants to be a member of the neighborhood gang and will offer to do whatever the older members ask. But institutions, like people, must have a clear identity, an awareness of self, a sense of purpose if they are to succeed. Until the community colleges gain a distinct identity, their effectiveness will inevitably be ambiguous. Unless taxpayers, legislators, faculty and administrators, students and parents have a clear concept of the institution, their present interest in the college will not be sustained.

But achieving and maintaining this sense of identity does not come easily. If identity is to be achieved by the community college, certain goals must be isolated and accepted as unique charges.

The colleges could, for example, vigorously pursue the study of instruction. Despite the magnitude of the American educational enterprise, surprisingly little is known about—and few agencies are systematically studying—the process of instruction. The two-year college is already more deeply involved in instruction than any other segment, and, although it does not presently have personnel with the requisite skills to carry on full-blown research, it could consciously study its instruction processes and products.

The community college might ask some of the following questions: Exactly what is being learned there? By whom? Are curricular and instructional practices as effective as they might be? For whom? And if not, why not? What forms of student achievement should be accepted as evidence that learning has occurred? If students were provided with sets of specific objectives upon entrance to the college, would their learning be enhanced? Would dropout rates be reduced? What else could be done to facilitate the process and guarantee the product? How can particular types of instructors be prepared to bring about learning? Which patterns of instructional supervision yield the best results? Should students be placed with instructors whose cognitive styles match their own? What qualifies a person to be a good teacher? Can everyone teach all types of learning objectives with equal facility? Are some instructors better at aiding recall, others at stimulating students to continue learning on their own? Are such attainments the result of discernible actions or of basic personality characteristics that lend themselves only to indirect measurement?

These questions represent directions for potentially fruitful study. Community colleges can profitably raise, dispute and tentatively answer them and, by merging studies of instructors and instruction, take steps toward institutional identity. To organize this type of inquiry means to continually redefine the institutional role. The more the institution tends to assess its own efforts, the more it must examine its own structures. As the junior colleges become the experimental education centers of higher education, they must abandon many of the institutional forms inherited from the universities and the secondary schools.

The two-year colleges are in unique positions to select, try out and demonstrate the efficacy of various instructional processes. They do not have to remain tied to the "standard academic model" that is, in fact, a quasi-imitation of the most reputable graduate schools. The two-year colleges might create professional models of good teaching, personal responsiveness and social and cultural enrichment in the community. Although a variety of teaching forms do not in themselves evidence a commitment to instruction as a central thrust, educational hardware and technological concepts may eventually push instruction—here defined as a deliberate sequence of events arranged so that learning occurs—to the fore.

The Carnegie Commission recommends greater institutional expansion—to 235 new community colleges by 1980, state-level planning, and hence, comprehensiveness in program coverage and ever-larger size. The American Association of Junior Colleges, the major professional association in the field, is similarly on the side of more and larger institutions. Both agencies foresee a time when nearly everyone continuing his or her education beyond a secondary school will begin in a two-year college.

Those who oppose these positions object to size, comprehensiveness and the tendency to reduce all educational experience to the lowest common denominator. They believe that state-level planning may well be undesirable because it tends to fix institutional role vis-a-vis other segments of higher education. They think community colleges might become more, rather than less, distinct; more, rather than less, specialized. And, above all, they feel each community college should develop an ethic of its own, its own identity, its own sense of central purpose; that the community and the individual students are less well-served by massive, bland carbon copies of the comprehensive high schools than they would be by small, unique institutions, each with its own mission.

When the community college was new and struggling for fiscal support, its leaders were quick to seize upon every apparent new function and offer to fulfill it. The time has come to face the fact that one institution cannot perform with equal facility the tasks that have been undertaken by this post secondary parvenu. Tension within an educational structure can be healthy if it leads to constant reexamination of function. But the obvious anomalies in the custodial, allocative and educative functions are not often examined. Decisions are made ad hoc, in a political arena; the philosophical bases to which they relate are left unstated.

The belief that human beings are innately different, that we need to protect the young, that the culture should be transmitted are the philosophical cornerstones of the public schools. But, for the community colleges, the issue should not be that people do or do not possess different capabilities; it is whether it is a school's business to attempt to find out, whether it can so determine without adversely affecting its instructional role. The issue is not that young people do or do not need to be kept off the streets and out of the labor force; it is whether or not a college can do this without untowardly affecting their growth. The question of whether or not people need to learn is not at issue; the true issue is the extent to which they can do so in an institution that has taken on so many variant functions. Perhaps the community needs other agencies to perform these functions. Perhaps not. It depends on one's view of society and one's faith in social institutions.

Are there better ways of performing the same functions? Ivan Illich has said that we are so captured by the schools that other schools are the only alternatives we can postulate. His society without schools has the appeal that most utopias possess; it also carries about the same likelihood of attainment. However, short of the "deschooling" called for by Illich, some viable alternatives to the present system can be formulated. These would be community colleges that freely acknowledge their real purposes, take on deliberate functions and make their institutional forms fit. They would still be subject to the ills of institutionalization, but at least they could be built feasibly within the existing social context. And they would be aware of their own identity and their distinct missions.

Several such plans have been proposed recently. One model has the community colleges attending strictly to teaching and learning on a defined outcomes basis, with the custodial and allocative functions abandoned along with the massive buildings and campuses. In this hypothetical college, a corps of professional instructors specify and articulate particularized learning objectives and prepare varieties of media to insure that all matriculants attain success. Not only have grading and other devices to sort people been abandoned; students are also involved in situations other than the classroom. Many of the objectives have the students working in the community and learning on their own. In addition, any time a person demonstrates ability to achieve the stated criteria regardless of where he learned the skill or concept—he is given credit and sent on.

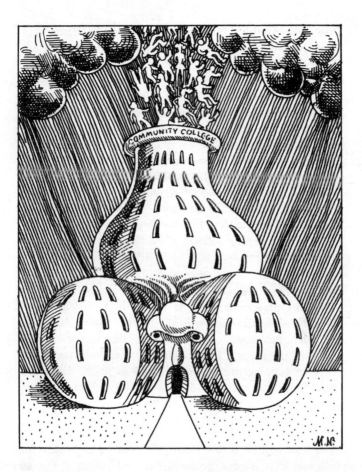

Another concept has the community college set up just to serve the guidance function. This agency has abandoned all pretense of formalized classroom instruction, offers only counseling services, psychological testing and information about various opportunities available for work, education and community involvement. The sole intent of the institution is to aid people in goal formulation and redirection.

Still another type of college could be a volunteer services agency that would coordinate a kind of domestic Peace Corps. Students would tutor in the lower schools, serve as recreation counselors and parks attendants, and have their work apprenticeship experiences coordinated. These experiences, in turn, become a new form of general education.

The custodial function is the most difficult to satisfy, primarily because a truly humanistic custodial institution is a contradiction on its face. Nevertheless, each community could support a place where young people would go to learn and develop in a non-pressure environment. It would offer concerts and films, records and paperback books, food and drink. It would have student-run shops, an open forum, the right of free assembly and would promise no wider goals. No one would be certified for attending.

The community college is not about to parcel out its present functions and separate itself into its component parts. Specialization demands deliberate vision, distinct identity, overt recognition of specific purpose. However, some sort of voucher plan is on the horizon which will stimulate alternative patterns of post secondary education. Not that increasing the demand for services inevitably increases the supply, but vouchering does hold the possibility of opening professional as well as public debate on what is being promised and what is being delivered by the college.

Institutionalism is insidious. We have a penchant for believing that once a problem has been defined and an institution created to deal with it, we no longer need to think about it. Education is not seen as a problem as long as schools are accessible and the community colleges thrive on this illusion. Their success is marked by their "providing opportunity for education." They are not called to account—nor do they hold themselves accountable—for the learning their students achieve. They allow all people to attend; perhaps that is all they really ever promised.

No screening device—whether birth, status, money or score attained on any test—has ever adequately predicted who will eventually perform society's tasks and attain personal satisfaction. Perhaps it is best to assume that, like any other trait, intelligence is normally distributed, and that by expanding the absolute numbers of people who feel they have had a chance to "be educated," the schools have done all that can be done. If this is so, the community colleges are a roaring success. Still, this view makes formal education seem a random event. One would hope we could do more with what we know about the processes of human learning.

A decade ago Clark Kerr postulated the "multiversity" concept to explain the university's broad involvement in social, political and economic affairs beyond its own walls. The drama of the multiversity is being re-enacted in the community college, but with two distinct differences. First, the community college has no centuries-old tradition of classical education that serves as an anchor. It does everything, takes on all responsibilities, promises to alleviate a variety of ills. It is thus like the multiversity without the restraining influence of the liberal arts tradition and, accordingly, is even more open to social and political suasion. Second, the community college has no cadre of professors, administrators or trustees who articulate alternative positions. Most of the people who speak from within the colleges offer the monolithic thesis of comprehensiveness. The advocates of finite goals presently are found on special task forces—such as the Newman Committee—or within the universities, or totally outside formal education.

The community colleges can do nothing about their lack of tradition. But they can now enhance their sense of identity by finding out for themselves what they are about. Then they can decide if being all things to all people—for a price—is indeed their true and ultimate mission.

A Psychoanalytic View of Learning

by Michael Maccoby

Because our schools have played a key role in forming the American character and will continue to do so, it is essential to understand the psychological principles underlying educational programs, and to develop ones that might guide future innovation towards forming productive character traits. With the goal of preparing students to succeed in a rapidly changing meritocracy, innovations in education often contribute to turning out compulsive winners and increasingly jaded consumers who have become cynical about learning. These young people may be expert at test taking but contribute little to the society and are often miserable because they feel centerless.

Parents and teachers justify these innovations in terms of test results, but unless they are evaluated in terms of character, their long range effects are likely to be negative. An example is the use of competitive games to speed up learning. Competitive behavior can be rooted in different character systems, ranging from a healthy pride in performance or workmanship to a predatory urge to destroy one's competition or a desperate need to be a winner in order to escape a feeling of worthlessness. Tests of ability, endurance and courage may help develop both the individual's potentialities and realism, and in athletics, speed, strength and skill provide opportunities for natural competition. However, it is another matter when all of learning is fitted into a game. Teaching through such games may inject rich doses of excitement and learning drive into many students who will as a result increase their test scores. But there is the danger of furthering the formation of an alienated-competitive character. Many of the children will become dependent on competition to stimulate them. Winning will become their real interest: they will prefer being first to understanding the nature of things. Because they will learn only what is necessary for success, their relatedness to knowledge will be superficial. Studies with children indicate that game-like competition not only narrows the breadth of their learning but can increase anxiety about losing, causing for some children paralyzing conflict and learning blocks. Many of the most independent, self-activating children need to work at their own pace and are upset by extrinsic rewards and punishment.

Another example of short-term learning and long-term character disorders is the extremely "stimulating" presentation of educational material which may indeed teach some things rapidly, but at the expense of developing the student's "activeness." Programs such as "Sesame Street" excite the children, but only recently has the question been asked (by the BBC) of what character traits are developed. Exciting learning through TV may further the consumer mentality in children, fostering their need for constant stimulation, for being entertained and "turned on." Other methods of learning the alphabet or numbers might take longer, but they might also emphasize *active* character traits, particularly concentration and the child's development of individual rhythms of work. We must consider the possibility that whatever the content of the programs, TV as a medium for teaching may have negative effects on character development, particularly if not combined with activating classroom discussion.

The examples given are related to two qualities of character—an alienated competitive attitude and the consumer mentality—which are often reinforced rather than confronted by the schools. Parents favor the use of any techniques that promise to speed up learning and get their children into college. *The New York Times* recently reported that a "teacher was ousted by fifteen sets of parents who were convinced that, after forty-five years of service, she was not prepared to handle 'Sesame Street' graduates." The teachers, for their part, also employ these techniques because they want to have an impact on students and need to show results. Furthermore, games and excitement save the teachers from guilty feelings of having to be "authoritarian" disciplinarians, and from having to know both their subject matter and their students thoroughly. However, the symptoms of anxiety and chronic boredom in young people make it necessary in higher education for teachers either to find new ways of "turning on" the students, or devoting a large part of their time to psychotherapy.

It is common to attribute the anxiety of the young to the spectre of nuclear war and the disintegration of the environment. These threats to existence cannot be discounted as sources of feelings of powerlessness and fear, and for young men, the war in Vietnam has been a further cause for unrest and uncertainty. Yet this explanation does not fully explain the intense anxiety of many students, and it focuses attention away from conditions in the schools which can be changed more easily.

The anxiety of high school students was documented most dramatically a few years ago in the film *Sixteen in Webster Groves*, prepared by the National Opinion Research Center and the CBS network. The filmmakers chose one of the richest middle-class communities in America and interviewed the high school students. At the time, in the middle-sixties, they found the students obsessed with fears about not making good enough grades or getting high enough test scores to go on to elite colleges and eventually find jobs that paid well enough to allow them to live in towns like Webster Groves, Lake Forest or Scarsdale. Only a few of the students were concerned about social issues, and most of them were outcasts.

Recently I spent the day with high school students in a suburb near Washington, D.C. In contrast to the Webster Groves of the mid-sixties, these young people were more conscious of the larger world outside of themselves and willing to work for progressive social change. But they too were anxious about success, fearful of letting down their parents and being labeled losers. Unlike the traditional academic program of Webster Groves, this high school encouraged independent study and social concern. Yet many students were doubtful whether they really cared about their individual projects or the community. They questioned their motives: perhaps they were acting because they thought leading colleges would favor the "involved student." The need to be "committed" seemed one more pressure to achieve. (It would be interesting to learn whether Webster Groves has moved in this same direction.) Given this anxiety, any new competitive pressures are likely either to overwhelm the student or move him further in the direction of cold, detached competitiveness and cynicism. Many cool competitors have overcome their anxiety at great emotional cost. Others, who cannot detach themselves from their feelings, drop out.

The other symptom, boredom, is a constant complaint of students, including some of those who succeed brilliantly on tests. At lectures in the leading universities one finds students sleeping, reading newspapers or day-dreaming. Sometimes this is a reaction to dull, alienated teachers. But often the students demand entertainment, particularly after having "put out" on their exams. The challenge and excitement needed to bring the class to life is not, however, intrinsic to discovery and understanding: it has little relation to love of learning. Rather, it is the stimulation necessary to whet the appetite of students who no longer care about the truth and can only be turned on by a good performance.

What kind of people do these anxious and bored students become? What is a compulsive winner or a consumer character? The description offered in this article is based on clinical work with college students by my colleagues and me. In psychoanalysis, we have explored the effects of their adaptation to competitive demands and consumer seductions. Some become frightened, confused and withdrawn. But others lose faith in life and have a diminished sense of self, leading them to worship secular idols, and unconsciously to pursue irrational goals. There is hardly a way to express the conflicts experienced by these students. The problem has to do with their goals and purposes. In medieval society, these character disorders might have been analyzed in terms of pride, greed, the temptation to sell the self for power or security and the feeling of being hopelessly damned. Today, even though such language describes experience, it sounds moralistic and pejorative rather than spiritually objective. On the one hand, the churches have for the most part stripped the experience from the concepts but retain official ownership of them. On the other hand, such a language clashes with the cool style which rejects the values of commitment and perfectibility such concepts imply. Yet some such concepts are needed to recognize and communicate the deepest conflicts that paralyze many young people and rob them of a chance for a productive life.

What we find through psychoanalysis is a weak, under-developed center in many students who have sought the alienated goals of the meritocracy. As one patient stated, "I experience a gaping hole where my self should be. Instead of interest, I feel hunger." Such students may be greedy for success or for stimulation because the potential source of energy centered in themselves has never been developed. They have learned to rev themselves up for tests, to become enthusiastic over what is expected from them, but left alone, they doubt their feelings and goals. Indeed the overriding goal is to do well and be thought well of. In some cases, overweening ambition or illusions of grandeur have been substituted for their real interests or a developing power over knowledge. Extreme ambition, often fed by parents and teachers, may be so frustrating that the gifted young person withdraws into fantasies or drugs.

Almost always, these patients begin to become aware in analysis that their lives have been in large part programmed for them, that they have never looked for their own goals or had the courage to pursue the latent interests not rewarded by parents, teachers or peers. Instead, they have let others decide for them: they have chosen goals to impress or to avoid ridicule rather than to realize inner vocations. For many, vocations are determined, if at all, by "objective" tests. Tastes are molded by the media. And political attitudes are formed by peer groups or the "youth culture." During the past decade, for example, more young people have been encouraged to take their values more seriously and translate them into political convictions. However, political relevance itself becomes a new form of oppression in some circles. Students become guilty about developing interests which are not commonly considered useful or socially beneficial. They are made to feel that the disciplined play of art and science is frivolous if not immediately "relevant" to social change. But the result of denying oneself is that the individual is cut off from the deepest wellsprings of creativity. Thus, those who seek therapy struggle to overcome their greed and illusions and to find in themselves the authentic interests so little developed by their home life and schooling.

Some psychiatrists think of the centerless individual as a positive development, particularly in contrast to their model of the uptight inner-directed individual. They argue that in a rapidly changing society, centerless people are the ones who adapt most successfully. This view is shared by such a creative social psychiatrist as Robert J. Lifton, one of the most sensitive interpreters of moral concerns and spiritual conflicts felt by college students. Lifton describes one variation of the centerless person as "protean man," who he argues substitutes "polymorphous versatility" for character. Lifton makes it a point to "stress that protean style is by no means pathological as such" and that it "may

well be one of the functional patterns of our day." Protean
man has no home or rootedness: he is fully committed to
nothing, and he substitutes many masks for an authentic
self. This is similar to the position of the late Frederick S.
Perls, founder of Gestalt Therapy and resident therapist at
Esalen. He wrote:

> Once you have a *character*, you have developed a
> rigid system. Your behavior becomes petrified,
> predictable, and you lose your ability to cope
> freely with the world with all your resources ... I
> say that the richest person, the most productive
> person, creative person, is a person who has *no*
> character.

But Lifton, Perls and others are romanticizing, providing an ideology for and finally advocating a character
type which they fail to analyze sufficiently. This modern
centerless character must be understood in relationship to
the social conditions that provide him his function. An
analysis by Erich Fromm in *The Sane Society* suggests that
the alienated centerless character tends to be developed by
conditions of bureaucratic industrialism. Fromm's description of the character who survives by selling an image of
himself is similar to Lifton's patient who wears many masks
and wonders if a self still exists. What Lifton fails to take
seriously is the fact that such a person is a patient. Even
though his character may be "functional," he has sought
treatment because he suffers. Perhaps the deepest suffering
for such a person, Fromm has written, is the shame of not
being oneself, of self-betrayal.

My experience with young people who saw themselves
in terms of a protean ideology was as psychoanalyst to a
commune. The group of college dropouts and street people
ranged in age from 17 to 25. They asked for a group
analysis because they were not living according to their
stated goals and values, which were to create a loving,
structureless environment. They wanted to be free of all
formal constraints and felt that they could be protean in

changing themselves to fit an ideal world. But they were not satisfied. Although they had gotten rid of all rules, authority, and commitments to individuals, they did not feel free and there was little trust or openness. While analysis in the usual sense was not possible, I agreed to join them in exploring why they were unable to achieve their goals. We met three hours a week for eight months. In the course of these meetings, the commune members became conscious of hidden goals to be fed and mothered. Some of them also became aware that while they had consciously rejected parental authority and values, they had substituted for them the equally rigid Ten Commandments of a "community parent" based on the dictates of the radical political movement. These included: exclusive relationships are like private property, bad; some drugs—grass and hash— are good but all needles are bad; women should not try to be beautiful unless they are born that way; having fun is suspect unless one can show it is politically useful. Once they realized that they had inescapably individual selves that were not infinitely malleable, the commune members saw themselves as passive conformists who were fearful of asserting individuality for fear of being abandoned by the mothering community.

A person with a strong sense of self may be predictable inasmuch as he has committed himself to people and ideals. However, it is naive to think that centerless individuals are not even more predictable. To foresee the behavior of the "marketing" character, one must study him in relationship to his social context, since he tends to act according to the demands of his market. Consider, for example, two types of the modern centerless character—the compulsive consumer and the game character—which are exaggerated products of character tendencies often reinforced in schools.

The compulsive consumer is typically depressed, though not so acutely that he always seeks psychiatric help; he compensates for this depression by a constant search for new forms of excitement and entertainment. These may include music, food, drugs, sex or politics. He hungers for novelty and stimulation: the action must be "new." Such a person may seem unpredictable because he or she is never committed to anyone or anything, but always ready to adopt the newest fad or style of life which promises to "turn him on." In some cases, the compulsive consumer's character may be rooted in a deeper psychopathology. Among these are the drug takers and alcoholics whose unconscious wish is to regress to a womb-like state of passive-certainty. Or the compulsive consumers of technology who seek a mechanical womb in which warmth, food and entertainment are all secured by pressing a button and there is no longer a need to wake up.

Another centerless person, the game character, comes to life in an atmosphere of risk and competition, of tests and challenges. His commitment is to a single goal: winning. Some gamesters are lone-wolf hustlers. However, the game character ·may also fit into the high pressure project atmosphere of many modern corporations. The game character type of manager is like a professional football quarterback and indeed thinks of himself in this way. He integrates a team of highly competitive specialists to act, if not cooperatively, at least interdependently. He plays by the rules, and tries to be fair in the meritocratic sense, since traditional prejudices and an autocratic attitude don't pay off. (Indeed, meritocratic-minded admissions committees at Harvard and probably elsewhere have made it a policy to accept compulsive winners, regardless of race or religion.)

The game character is a person who derives his identity from his role or position on the team. Other than to win, his goals tend to be vague. Recently, I interviewed a highly successful industrial manager who admitted that he was no longer interested in his work. He had proved himself a winner, but he felt empty and without any goal in life. Once he stopped the compulsive activity and faced the meaninglessness of constantly competing, he experienced the depression due to the lack of a center.

A future society in which such character types are not only functional but dominant would be like Kurt Vonnegut's social nightmare, *Player Piano*, in which a small, highly trained and hard-working managerial class runs the automated factories while the majority of powerless consumers live off the dole. But if the centerless "protean" individual has been functional before, there is no guarantee that he will be in the future. It is exactly the pressure to negate the self that makes people dissatisfied today about work. This is the case not only for such highly trained individuals as engineers in large corporations, but also for blue-collar workers. Recent studies show an increasing demand, especially on the part of younger people, for work that requires more independence, judgment and craftsmanship.

Furthermore, the development of technology may make it possible to replace the most uncreative professional as well as manual work with computerized machines. Even today, managers in some of the most advanced technological corporations consider the most valuable workers the ones who are able to think for themselves, yet work cooperatively on projects they consider worthwhile. Such individuals also tend to be the ones who are most free to enjoy their leisure without a compulsive search for excitement, because they are interested in both learning and disciplined self-expression.

One of the most creative tasks of the future could be to redesign both industrial and bureaucratic work so that instead of requiring alienated individuals, the work stimulated the development of the self and favored active individuals. Such an organization of work would imply not only industrial democracy and a form of workers' management, but also the restructuring of the work groups themselves so as to eliminate purely rote tasks and hierarchical structures. The experiments by Robert Ford in the Bell System show a direction for such restructuring.

It should be added that the United States is not alone in suffering the character disorders of bureaucratic industrialism. A recent speech by Dr. Pyotr L. Kapitsa, the

Soviet physicist, describes the centerless, consumer mentality as increasingly evident in the Soviet Union. Because
of such people, he considers society unprepared to make
profitable use of the material wealth and leisure time with
which it has been endowed by the scientific-technological
revolution. Dr. Kapitsa concludes that "the problem before
education is therefore not only to provide man with the
broad knowledge necessary to become a useful citizen, but
to develop the independence of thought needed to develop
a creative understanding of the world around him."

How can education be directed toward the development
of the student's core? Does it mean returning to the
Protestant Ethic and rugged individualism? But the society
of farmer-frontiersmen and independent businessmen that
produced such character traits has largely disappeared.
There are still sub-cultures of artisans and small shop-
keepers where children grow up with the emotional attitudes that support values of stubborn independence, self-
abnegation, compulsive work and saving. Many of the most
productive industrial engineers have these traits. This character is also found more in students at colleges which
service ethnics with College Board scores about 500 than at
the more selective colleges. But in our present day
affluent society the consistent trend in employment is
toward organization, in service industries and professions as
well as in industry and government. Furthermore, powerful
cultural forces have undermined the traditional hoarding
attitudes that are the foundation of the Protestant ethic
and rugged individualism. The most important of these are
advertising, the allure of the shiny products themselves, and
the sexual revolution which does much to loosen the
uptight self-protectiveness that holds the hoarding character
together.

The real character alternatives in the post-industrial
organizational society are either variations on the centerless, alienated character or an individuated productive-
cooperative character. Fromm defined *productive character*
as the person able to use his powers and realize the
potentialities inherent in him. This implies an individuated

person, one who is free to think for himself and who is guided by reason, since he can make use of his powers only if he knows what they are, how to use them and what to use them for. Productiveness means that the individual is centered, that he experiences himself as the subject of his powers, that he is not alienated from them, i.e., that they are not masked from him and transferred to an idolized person, team or institution. Fromm points out that productiveness implies an attitude to all of life. The productive person has "soul"; he gives birth to his own faculties and gives life to persons and things. He is also responsibly related to persons, things and ideas, in contrast to the centerless gamester or the narcissistic super-individualist or hipster.

Educational methods alone cannot guarantee the development of the productive character. However, it may be possible to chart a direction for educational programs to improve social character. As a start, there are four general principles that if developed by teachers would further education that strengthens the self. These principles may seem obvious to those teachers who are already sensitive to the issues discussed here. However, a number of teachers have encountered opposition from school administrations or parents when they have introduced innovations with the aim of strengthening the child's self. A coherent explanation of their purpose, in terms of principles, might have helped overcome some of the resistance. In stating the principles, the details of workable programs can only be pointed to. A great deal of research and development needs to be done.

The first principle is that *schooling should provide the discipline needed for the development of the self.* This requires first of all that the teachers know the authentic interests and potentialities in their students that could be developed, since "interests" claimed by students sometimes are merely responses to fads. (For teachers to develop knowledge about authentic interests and vocations would require changes in the content of most psychology programs.) It also requires a careful definition of "discipline." Traditionally we have thought of the concept in terms of "orderly conduct," "control," "obedience," or, as a verb, "to punish." However, discipline also means "training that perfects," and it is only in this sense that we can speak of aiding the student to develop his powers to express himself, to pursue knowledge and wisdom with love, and to envision more joyful ways of living.

In *Zen in the Art of Archery*, Eugen Herrigel describes a discipline which gives meaning to tedious learning in terms of the ultimate goal of spontaneity. In a similar way, children can understand the purpose of having to work at elementary mathematics or music not as a means to get ahead, but as a discipline for being able to make work

into serious play. In a recent article, "The Three C's and Discipline for Freedom" (*The School Review*, February 1971) I have described the discipline of the self as including the ability to concentrate, to think critically and to communicate (to express oneself and to listen). Such discipline develops naturally if rooted in a strong sense of self. A program initiated by Mrs. Elton Warren in the Bronx appears an example of a technique which sets this direction for young children, who are helped to find their own rhythms. Mrs. Warren reports that "once the child finds his own rhythm, he is better able to hear those of others."

The discipline of the self, if developed in childhood, arms a person to resist the organized distractions of the environment, equips him to doubt and unmask deceptive appearances, and emphasizes that the quality of his relatedness to others improves with systematic work.

The second principle is that *education should reinforce the natural development of the self.* This means that educational programs should be informed by continual study of the psychosocial and physical developmental process. Studies of human development sometimes isolate one aspect of development from the whole. Recent critics have pointed out that programs for cognitive development generally ignore emotional growth. But those who speak for "the whole child" themselves overlook crucial questions. Jean Piaget's early work on the moral judgment of children and other studies indicate that at the time children enter school, they are also struggling with a developing sense of self and with a new potential to be critical toward authority. How do techniques geared toward speeding the child's "cognitive" development or emotional expressiveness affect the child's character development? How do they come to grips with egocentrism and competitiveness?

If the adolescent's goal is to individuate himself, to become an individual, he finds little help from his schooling. Real *individuation* is a life-long process that requires independence, discipline and commitment; to become "oneself" is a work of art. In contrast, *individualism* is a broad concept that covers many different character-types, varying from the stubborn rebel to the passive consumer who buys his own thing. The normal adolescent would welcome a deeper understanding of individuation and what it requires. Instead, he often falls into the illusion of individualism through wearing certain clothes, listening to certain kinds of music or adopting unique mannerisms.

The same problems confront adolescents in high school and entering college. Erik Erikson's studies have shown that this period is a time of conflict, of struggle between "ego identity" (centeredness) vs. role diffusion and later, between narcissism and deeper relatedness. While Erikson's work is frequently cited by educators, we know little about methods to further a healthy sense of the individual self. One suggestion in this direction is David Riesman's idea of encouraging college students to develop aspects of themselves which they avoid because of fear they will not do well or look good. In some new therapeutic-educational approaches, emotions are emphasized at the expense of intellectual, moral and spiritual concerns; some overly facile encounter group methods feed adolescent narcissism without developing the means for deeper relatedness to others. In contrast, Rolando Weissman, who is studying psychoanalysis and social psychology with me, has taught experimental courses with the goal of developing psychospiritual consciousness. His work suggests that high school seniors can learn to understand symbolic language, including dreams, in such a way as to increase their consciousness about the structure of the world and their own specific role in it. Most important, the analysis of dreams makes the students aware of pressures and impulses to self betrayal, and this knowledge gives them an awareness of significant decisions they must make.

The third principle is that *in teaching a constant effort must be made to clarify the purpose of study and make explicit the values implied.*

Once goals and values are made explicit, the student is able to decide for himself whether or not to accept them. If they are not explicit, he tends to be mystified. The professor who honestly confronts his students doesn't present the choice of areas of study as representing "the field" but as a particular approach to knowledge which has ascertainable implications for man and represents a particular set of priorities. Some of the most productive student protest has clarified and opposed hidden purposes and values in the university which have supported militarism or the megamachine.

The new PhD program of the Institute for Policy Studies and the Union Graduate School in Washington has built into it the principle that the student must not only learn to examine the human and social implications of innovative projects but also to accept responsibility for them. While this program defines its purposes in terms of social action, it is sometimes necessary to repeat that there are, of course, other valid purposes for studying the arts and sciences. A valid purpose implies that learning is not alienated from the self but rather is an expression or fulfillment of one's deepest interests, principles and convictions. Once purposes are fully analyzed, then individuals who share them can join together in projects which do not require the loss of self in order to achieve cooperation. Otherwise, cooperation must be achieved by force or seduction.

The analysis of purpose needs to be made continually, although not obsessively. Purposes must be re-evaluated and renewed to keep them from changing direction or going underground. Psychoanalysis provides considerable clinical evidence that irrational purposes are often like secret plots disguised by cover stories. These purposes can only be maintained if they remain hidden; in the light of reason, they are seen as mad. In contrast, rational purposes rooted in love of life do not have to be unconscious, because they are usually shared by others.

The final principle is that *teaching techniques should develop the student's activeness.* If we do not use games, TV presentations and other exciting motivations, how is it possible to teach those students who seem to resist more traditional methods? Would teachers have to be tough disciplinarians? The answer is to be found in the testimony of many non-authoritarian, stimulating teachers who have activated students by centering the learning process in the child's own experience. Joseph Featherstone has described this method as practiced in the United Kingdom. Sylvia Ashton-Warner, Herbert Kohl and others have demonstrated that an active interest in reading and writing is developed when the themes are generated by the students. The principle of "activeness" implies self-direction and purpose. In *The Revolution of Hope* Fromm makes it a central principle of humanistic management. It has been applied to education by Paolo Freire, who contrasts the active method of dialogue and problem posing to the passive "banking" and "nutritional" approaches to teaching. In the banking approach, knowledge is deposited in students to be withdrawn on order in tests; the nutritional approach means feeding the students the knowledge the teacher considers lacking. In both methods, the teacher's authority is based fundamentally on his position in the hierarchy. In contrast, dialogue implies that teacher and student are both seeking the answer to a question that interests them. The authority of the teacher rests on his knowledge of theory, methods and research findings relevant to answering that question. Dialogue is not a magical form that replaces all lectures or learning from books. Rather, it is a way of teaching students to think in terms of problems, to take seriously their puzzlement and to consider alternatives to things as they are.

The student begins to become more active as he learns to translate his questions into scientific or bibliographic research. A few years ago, I joined Professors Douglas Dowd, an economist; Marie Augusta Neal, a sociologist; and John Rensenbrink, a political scientist, in developing and presenting an introductory course in the social sciences that incorporated the principle of dialogue and problem posing. (See Michael Maccoby, "The Cornell Introductory Course in the Social Sciences." *Harvard Educational Review,* Sum-

mer 1967). The title of the course was "Why Are There
Poor People in a Rich Society like the United States?," a
question that none of the professors could easily answer
and each considered important to investigate. The course
not only invited the students to ask their own questions,
but also presented the example of the dialogue among the
professors who had to confront their own differences and
biases. In the course of study, the students also began to
face themselves, to ask whether they cared about the
question or whether they were only interested in being
entertained or in getting good grades.

These principles of teaching are meant to provide a
psychological basis for innovation in schooling. They require, of course, teachers who strive to be themselves, to
combine love of learning with respect for the self in others.
However, even if these principles were adopted and applied
by productive teachers, all the students would not change
instantly, since the educational system is only one part of
the character-forming culture. In many schools, among
them some of the most "innovative" ones, strong resistance would be expressed by both students and teachers.
Many would worry that such emphasis on the self would
not prepare students for entrance exams and college admission. On the other side, there would be complaints that any
discipline is oppressive and that students should just learn
what they wish. The latter argument both ignores the need
for structured learning and the power of family and the
media. By the time they reach school, many children have
been made to doubt their perceptions and interests; unless
teachers affirm and help to develop their potentialities,
these students will be likely to follow the going fads with
no chance to become individuated. As to the worry about
college admission, this depends in large part on the responsiveness of higher education.

Will the schools and universities reinforce the dehu-
manizing alternatives of post-industrial social character, or
consciously adopt the goal of developing a discipline for the
productive character?   □